Social Selling:

*How Direct Selling Companies Can Harness the Power of Connectivity...
and Change the World*

Jonathan Gilliam

Foreword by Richard Brooke

Library of Congress Cataloging-in-Publication Data
Gilliam, Jonathan.
Social selling: how direct selling companies can harness the power of
connectivity...and change the world / Jonathan Gilliam.—1st ed.
  1. Business & Economics : E-Commerce - Internet Marketing. 2.
     Business & Economics : Marketing – General 3. Business & Eco-
     nomics : Marketing – Multilevel

ISBN 978-0-9856216-0-5

Printed in the United States of America

Interior Design by Clark Kenyon

Cover Art Design by Budi Setiawan

10 9 8 7 6 5 4 3 2

To my family and friends, and especially to Anabelle, Ava and Eden, whose arrival into this world gave me life too.

Catch my kiss.

Preface

THIS BOOK IS WRITTEN FOR THOSE direct selling executives and leaders who have a sincere affinity for the people that make this such a great industry, the field sales force, and for those who are sentimental for the past yet who embrace an unknown future, leaving the door open to new ideas and viewpoints. For you, I offer this interpretation of What It All Means.

Many people helped in the making of this book. Friends of mine who are also authors warned me this project would be all consuming, and you were right. To my wife Leanna, thank you for your love, patience and support.

Thank you to our awesome clients, a collection of some of the industry's best companies. Also thanks to our employees and partners, especially to Maria Duron and our social maven team for their contributions. You are the best social media team this industry has to offer.

A big, would-not-be-here-if-not-for-you thanks to the companies and executives who trusted us in our early days and helped build our firm to where it is today.

Thanks also to Karen Clark, Michelle Larter and all my friends, industry consultants and suppliers who trust us to take care of their clients, and the wonderful direct selling professionals and field reps who continue to support us and the firm. This really is the best industry in the world, and I'm truly proud to be a part of it.

Author's Note: This industry uses many different terms and titles. For the purposes of consistency I use "direct selling" network marketing and multi-level marketing interchangeably. I also use "distributor" to cover field sales representatives, consultants, associates, members and the myriad of names used to indicate the independent sales reps in the field.

Foreword

IN 1995 A FEW OF MY sales leaders invited me to a high level secret meeting. They proposed that we start selling our products via a "Web Site" by advertising in some sort of digital yellow page book. They wanted me to invest $200,000 in creating this web site and another $100,000 in the advertising. They wanted to use our trade name in some kind of web address…www. com or something. I thought they were involved in "creative avoidance"…How not to sell and recruit by focusing on the next big thing. I passed.

One of the luckiest (or smartest) things I ever did though was give them the use of the name contractually with the right to take it back if this harebrained next big thing ever really was the next big thing. Getting it back three years later when their initial attempts failed was a good thing.

Mankind has invented more things and processes in the last 50 years than in its 50 million year history. And we are on course to do so again in the next five. Why? In a word, *collaboration*. Fifty years ago if you were noodling an idea you were noodling it by yourself or maybe with a couple of schoolmates. Maybe there were a couple of books that would help flush out the pieces of the idea once you read the *whole* book.

Today if you are creating something new you are collaborating with the brightest minds not just in your dorm room but in your universe...all seven billion of them. And of course not just them but every mind that had anything to say about your idea worth writing down in the last 2000 years. We are collaborating with our entire planet and our entire history all because of linking together a couple of ideas...The modern computer. Data transmission. The Internet. BOOM. Today those three ideas can come together in an instant...one plus one equals thirty.

Which ones of us are so naïve to think that the Internet is it...the last big thing in creativity? Think not. Something is coming.

Maybe it is social media. Why would we think that? When is the last time the world was graced with an entire new country, hell a new continent? Facebook has redefined the concept of community. First they were a community without borders, then a small country, then the third largest country in the world—without even including the largest country in the world, I cannot even quote how many "citizens" Facebook has because the quote will be grossly out of date in a year.

Oddly (because I like to think I am not stupid), I had the same reaction to suggestions that we get "on facebook" and "start tweeting". How could what I had for breakfast do anything to drive business?

Now, I personally have almost 5000 "friends" and 16,000 people that have "clicked" that they care about my tweets. And I have no idea what I am doing. Worse yet I don't even *want* to do it.

Here is an example: I have in the last two years regularly posted thousands of things on Facebook and twitter…things I carefully and sincerely thought would move people, inspire them, interest them in my path and help them on their own paths. Some of my most profound posts get zero response. To date the number one post was about the morning I got up late for a meeting, couldn't find my glasses because they were on my head and went down to the hotel meeting room with mismatched dress shoes. BOOM. A tsunami of inspired responses and shares.

The business and social world is a rapidly changing landscape. It is like we drove a familiar road to a family vacation every year. But then one year a natural disaster of epic proportions had changed the entire landscape…no familiar roads or landmarks. The smart thing to do to save time and capital would be to hire a guide…someone with a 40,000 ft view of the terrain, someone that had navigated it many times already.

Jonathan Gilliam is one such guide. I have spent 35 years in the Direct Sales profession, much of that time studying people, thought processes, attitudes and character. There are precious few professionals that have ever captured my imagination like Jonathan. He is bright, experienced with success and failure, forward thinking, somewhat practical and yet ambitious in a big way. He gets this Social Media thing. If I could entice him into being part of my companies I would give him a significant piece of them just to have his vision and creativity on board forever.

I don't know what I don't know on this one. And that is a dangerous place from which to lead. Unless of course you know it, and plug the hole.

What I do know is that we in this great industry of direct selling or network marketing or whatever it's called in five or ten years are in for epic changes in our social—and therefore business—landscape every few years from here on out. And a Harvard Business School sheepskin is not going to cut it. We have to get out in front of this or at the very minimum hang on tight to its tail. The corporate grave yard is littered with know-it-alls like me.

In closing, my secret wish is that we create, innovate and breakthrough so many times in the next decade that we implode into a soulful realization that we all long for the simpler, slower, more private and intimate times of our parents and grandparents era.

When the traditional Tupperware Party is the next big thing.

Richard Brooke
Founder & CEO, Oxyfresh Worldwide, Inc.
Chief Visionary Officer, 21Ten
Board Member, Direct Selling Association
Author, Trainer and Coach

Contents

Contents

Introduction

Social Selling: Connecting, Not Collecting

social selling [soh-shul] [sel-ing] noun

*The natural evolution of the direct selling
business model, driven by social media
and mobile technologies*

RECENTLY A PROSPECTIVE SOCIAL MEDIA CLIENT asked me, "How much do you tweet?"

I almost immediately noticed what the client didn't ask, rather than what he did. Not "What do you tweet about?" or "What's your ratio of informational tweets to selling tweets?" or "Who do you tweet to?" He didn't even ask, "What's the most effective time of day to tweet?"

My mental response was also immediate. This particular executive didn't understand what's really important about social media. If you're going to use social media platforms like Twitter or Facebook, you need to know how to use them. Having high popular-

1

ity scores and hundreds of tweets every day doesn't mean you're being effective at the *business* of social media (and believe me, it is a business). The number of tweets – or time of day, or number of followers, or even the ability to pack full humor into 140 characters – doesn't make you good at it.

It's not about the number of tweets or even the number of followers. I would rather have one hundred interested, interactive friends and followers than one thousand static ones.

This prospect had the wrong idea about what social media actually is, for both the world at large and for his business. Rather than a place to add as many names as possible to a list, it's about engagement and relationships.

It's a place to *connect*, not collect.

I wish I could say that this was the first time I'd seen otherwise very astute business people apply old school metrics or expectations to the new world of social media. These kinds of "quantity versus quality" misconceptions are common, and spotlight a real disconnect between the business of social media and its perception in the direct selling community. Many of the most intelligent, effective people in this industry don't quite yet understand how to use social media effectively – and efficiently – to connect to the rest of the world, or more importantly, what it means to our cherished ways of doing business.

So why do we seem timid when it comes to social media? What are we so afraid of? Why, when we specialize in selling person-to-person and smile-to-smile, does the prospect of social media seem to intimidate us so much?

From a business perspective, we should be in lockstep with Facebook, mastering Twitter, straight up dominating LinkedIn, and all over Pinterest, and whatever the next big social media platform is. We should be completely capitalizing on this phenomenon of people being so instantly connected. Of having access to thousands of people we would never have accessed in the past.

Because of the traditionally social aspects of our business model, our industry has a chance to become the commerce leader in this media. Instead, many companies seem to lurk in the shadows, occasionally tweeting their latest promotions, casually updating a lackluster Facebook page, and ignoring Pinterest and the vast array of tools that could support their businesses in unimagined ways.

> **66** *The better your company is at social media, the more successful your field will be, which will advance the entire industry.* **99**

Most direct selling companies are missing out on the powerful connections and tremendous company growth that social media offers. In turn, their independent sales field turns out volumes of mediocre, ineffective and even reckless social media content, all of which affect their companies and the industry at large.

The better your company is at social media, the more successful your field will be, which will advance the entire industry.

This is why I wanted to write this book. To help the companies that help so many people.

I'm Jonathan Gilliam, Founder and CEO of Momentum Factor, a marketing and management firm exclusively serving direct selling companies.

I believe in this industry and its power to help millions of people, and I do everything I can to see the industry—and the people and companies who power it—succeed.

In this book, I'm going to introduce you to the best of both the social media and direct selling worlds. I call it Social Selling. And much of it should feel familiar to you.

In my experience, no one knows more about the core functionality of Social Selling—incentives, systems, and how to appeal to people on a personal level—than direct selling industry executives. That means you. Social Selling shouldn't be a new or different concept for you. Direct selling and Social Selling are two sides of the same coin. This industry is practically synonymous with self-motivation and individualism as well as its *culture of community*. Not just in the field, but amongst the companies themselves. It's the corporate philosophy throughout the industry to help each other when and where we can.

When I was starting my first direct selling company, I was taken aback by the offers of help and support I received–from my *competitors*.

It was something I hadn't experienced in my previous career; competitors were enemies to be outsmarted and subverted. They weren't supposed to take after-hours calls about which computer vendors were best. Sure, there are jealousies and tough competition in any industry, but it's different here. My friend Kerry Shea Penland, CEO of All'Asta, was amazed at the level of support she encountered when she first entered the industry. "I had the CEOs of some of the world's best known companies giving me advice that I know saved me years of mistakes and frustration. I would not have made it out of the gate but for the kindness of competitors."

The people of this wonderful industry are what drew me to it and continue to make me excited to get out of bed every day, galvanized and inspired.

Other industries come to business from a "me first" attitude; we're more "we first." Many of us got into this business by accident, but at some early point in our direct selling executive careers someone reached out to help and we realized that we would never go back to regular, mainstream corporate life again. It would seem so…impersonal.

No one could stay in this business very long without a natural affection for everyday people. Sure, there are plenty of opportunists in the industry (we all know a few). But I don't believe that one can achieve sustainable success in this industry without a sincere and abiding love for people.

Why should our social media experience, as an industry, be any different? What's incredible about social media is that our companies can now reach untold numbers of people via technology. We can reach each other in ways not possible before. We have instant communication and teamwork at our fingertips, and still get to hang on to our core values as an industry.

But we need to do it right if it's going to work. We can improve the lives of millions more today via our messages, our innovative products, social giving programs, and our education in entrepreneurship, leadership and personal development at a scale unimaginable a few years ago. And as we collect the opportunities technology gives us we shouldn't lose sight of the real goal that Social Selling helps us achieve – connections with people.

Together, we're going to take what we already know how to do – sell to and through people, directly – and apply those very same skills to social media to master something I call "Social Selling."

And it's going to get easy, I promise. Soon, it'll become second nature. You'll wonder in ten pages or less, why it took you so long to realize the power of Social Selling. I'm guessing that you'll be itching to ramp up your company's social media effort in no time.

The purpose of this book is to describe and explain the new world we find ourselves in, cut through the noise and show you how to leverage the massive opportunity that awaits us in the new, connected and mobile world.

So if you're ready, let's jump in and get started.

Chapter 1

The Social Media/Direct Selling Mash-Up

"Creativity is just connecting things." ~
Steve Jobs

When someone is introduced to your company's direct selling opportunity, what is the first thing they do? Visit your website? Not likely. Call your 800 number? Not unless there's a problem.

They check with their social networks. They check Google. Maybe even right then and there, from their phone. They will try to identify people they know who know you and your company.

That is the world we are in—one where the rules have changed. The old methods dozens of industries relied upon for hundreds of years have been rendered obsolete. New pathways have been carved for many. For others, their businesses slowly ebbed and dried up.

Why should direct selling get a pass from these changes? The truth is, we haven't. Our industry has changed, just as the others have. Not as dramatically (thankfully) as some, but it's happened.

The Big Mash-up

The direct selling industry is being "Mashed-up". No that's not some new potato-related network marketing opportunity. Mash-up is a relatively new term describing a creative combination or mixing of content from different sources. Mash-ups are enabled by technology: take several songs and blend them together to make a new song, that's a mash-up. A web mash-up might overlay digital maps with crime statistics to produce a crime map.

The advent of social media and mobile has mashed-up our industry into something new and unique, and not as recognizable as before.

Look around. Networkers are *different*. Recruiting is *different*. Communications are vastly *different*.

Minerva Worldwide attempts to make Social Selling a reality

Think this old school industry is threatened by Social Selling? Not for those who eagerly embrace it.

Take one of our clients, Minerva Worldwide. They recently undertook an ambitious and potentially game-changing effort to form a new kind of company, one that not only uses social media to market their products but makes social selling a part of the offering.

CEO John Gustin describes their thinking as they formed the company. "When we were initially coming up with our concept, we took a good look at how online and social technologies had changed network marketing as a model. Recruiting had become easier in some ways, but harder in others. The field's behaviors were morphing along with technology" he said. "We knew that whatever we did, it had to leverage social media and search marketing as primary drivers. So we looked for the areas of the greatest reach, scale and growth potential, and then worked to figure out how to bring them all together."

With an understanding of how sharable content reaches people and proliferates, Minerva started with the content first. They decided to build a destination site for diet, health and beauty. They signed "Dancing with the Stars" TV host Brooke Burke as spokesperson and hired venerable Hollywood producers, writers and editors to create volumes upon volumes of interesting, sharable content.

Next, they built an ecommerce platform and shopping mall filled with products related to health, diet and beauty. At the same time, they created a full-fledged traditional network marketing company, MinervaRewards.com and enrolled well-known leaders and networkers to bring in the field as founding members.

As a result, networkers who join the company get their own personalized ecommerce store and lots of content to share with their social networks, along with training in how to market themselves correctly online.

In theory, the social sharing of Minerva content should lead to traffic to the member's website and ostensibly to sales. Members use online content to "market" their business and are not bound by some of the traditional network marketing hurdles.

The model combined the advantages of first-rate content, affiliate marketing, ecommerce and network marketing into one offering with multiple streams of revenue for their reps, creating a new kind of hybrid company.

By focusing on the elements of what already works in social media and online marketing, Minerva may have cracked the code on Social Selling.

This certainly doesn't mean we are at a loss, or that we need to start packing it in. Not by any means. We can benefit – even wildly so—from the changes forced on us by this new connected world.

Probably the most important thing to establish at the outset of this book is *we already have the advantage.* What defines our whole industry is the social nature of the direct sale, and that gives us a terrific edge over larger, retail-based businesses which depend upon advertising and immediate convenience to attract buyers.

We already know how to make connections, build

relationships, and cultivate friends. In a certain sense we invented social commerce. Just think of it: Facebook and Pinterest have amazing parallels with companies like Mary Kay and Pampered Chef, whether it is readily apparent or not.

Now you may be thinking, "C'mon, Jonathan! I may know how to cut perfect commission checks or ship product or even inspire people to better themselves. But I don't have the first clue how to post, poke, tweet, tut, or link myself to anything! I have to ask my kids to help me order stuff online, and I'm still not so sure about putting my credit card number on the InterWebs. How am I supposed to create social strategies when I can barely turn on my computer?"

I get it, I do, and we've all had frustrating moments with new technology, but it's important not to psych ourselves out of the game. With the help, direction, and advice of people just a little more attuned to the current technological winds, smooth sailing is easily within our grasp.

Perhaps a metaphor might help. We already know the language of Social Selling. We know how to joke, tell stories, introduce ourselves, share our hopes and dreams and frustrations, and most importantly listen to people who often start out as total strangers to us. We know how to anticipate needs and concerns, allay anxieties, and help the people understand how our companies can transform their lives.

There is certainly an age element here. Boomers

and even Gen X'ers (of which I am a proud, latchkey-carrying member) are immigrants to the world of social media. We moved here, but we didn't grow up here. All this technology can feel foreign to us, but we work to learn the local customs, and the good news? We direct sellers already know the language.

Social Selling is our native tongue, and it's the social part that will put us in the best stead.

How Social Selling Is Not So New for Direct Sellers

The technology of Social Selling may be new, the apps might be new, the tools we use to engage may be new, but the concept itself is ages old. And it's familiar territory for us.

Consider the following:

1. **Relationships have always mattered.** At its heart, Social Selling is about creating relationships. So is direct selling. From its very inception, our industry has always been built on person-to-person relationships.

2. **We've always trusted our friends.** Chances are good that you bought your last big screen TV, video game or DVD on the recommendation of a friend, coworker, family member, or neighbor. The fact is that you trust those you know over those you don't know. Sure, we may be lulled into the occasional purchase when outgunned by a professional, yet in most cases we prefer to

turn to our friends first, and traditional media – ads, fliers, sales, etc. – second or third.

3. **Share and share alike.** We have always shared, from our earliest days in this industry; we've shared stories, tips, advice, and company gossip. There may be new ways to share now, but why we do it – even with whom we do it– is centuries old.

4. **Technology changes, people don't.** If you look closely at Facebook, Twitter, Pinterest, LinkedIn and even YouTube, you'll see people basically doing the same things they've always done – gossiping, ranting, sharing, caring, cheering, jeering, and pooh-poohing. Nowadays, they're simply doing it online rather than over the backyard fence

5. **Look at the terminology.** "Friends." "Followers." "Share." "Like." Sound familiar? It should – it's the language of direct selling as well.

6. **Dialogue, not monologue.** Most people think of social media as a one-way, top-down conversation, and therefore often fail at it. Ads, infomercials, product placement – these have been around forever. Unfortunately many take this old-fashioned theology and apply it to newfangled technology, with lackluster results. In social media, marketing can only work (and does work) if it's natural and not forced.

7. **We are curious creatures.** This tendency to 'window shop' propels Facebook, Twitter, Pin-

terest and all the rest forward. We are naturally inquisitive, always have been.. Social media gives us a way to satisfy our natural curiosity. Learning about and marketing to that curiosity will help you master Social Selling from the inside out.

8. **We love immediate gratification.** One of the primary benefits of online technology is its speed. No ringing phone, no waiting around, no hemming and hawing ... just type it in and get a response, lickety split. We can generally find any topic we want – new TV ratings, celebrity gossip, career advice, you name it – in any forum the minute we go looking for it. With social and mobile technology, direct sellers can quickly demonstrate how people can reach their goals with our offerings. Faster is indeed better.

9. **We all want a voice.** A major driver of social media growth comes from a basic human need to express ourselves. From the earliest caveman drawings to singing in the shower to shouting it from the rooftops, we have always wanted to be heard. Social Selling gives us all a voice. If we learn to say the right things at the right times, to the right people, our message can be heard around the world.

All of these points happen to fall right into the direct selling core competencies. We are really, really good at making people feel welcome, at forging relationships, at turning friends into business associates and business associates into friends.

This means that you already know how to do it. The next step is mastering how to blend your real world social expertise with social media.

Social Selling Starts With You

By now it should be clear how valuable these tech-

"Tarzan no want computer."

nologies can be to your business and why it is vital that your business begin Social Selling if it has not already, and beef up its program if it already has.

I say that not because of the money to be made (although if you do it correctly the revenue and success will be there) but because Social Selling is so right for you, for us, as individuals and an industry.

It starts with you. If you have a Facebook page set up, begin using it to connect with others like you. If you're talking about tweeting, you learn more about how to tweet effectively and responsibly. Learn how Pinterest works by doing it yourself, first. This way you will at least be a fluent foreigner in a strange land, and not the one that just refuses to learn the new language no matter how advantageous it would be or how many doors it would open.

So what does the direct selling/social media mash-up mean for our industry?

Put on those shades, the future's looking bright.

Chapter 2

The Selling Future is Ours to Win

"All great changes are preceded by chaos."
~ Deepak Chopra

MOST DIRECT SELLERS "HAVE" A FACEBOOK page but that's about it. They don't get results from them, because results take time and money. They figure that if they've set it up, then the people will come. Hey, at least they have one, right?

When customers don't come in hordes as the company might have hoped, they move on to more "pressing" matters, and their efforts become a static testament to mediocrity. Ultimately their pages and profiles typically succumb to a deluge of self-promoting third parties and opportunists who "adopt' their brand and good name. End of story.

The same goes for Twitter: companies set up a Twitter profile, but then get bogged down by the hash tags, the timelines, and the time it takes to genuinely communicate and make connections through this platform. So they don't take the time to learn how to use the media. Then they say, "I don't have time for this; I have a real job." And that's the end of their Twitter page.

> **❝** *Use what you've already learned about direct selling and apply it to social media.* **❞**

The trouble is that for them to succeed at their "real job" they need to figure out how to make these other things work.

So take another look; let's revisit those Facebook pages and Twitter accounts again. Look at them as opportunities, not obstacles, and I think you'll have a better appreciation of what I'm talking about. Use some of the tools and paths I present in this book, and look for ways to utilize those pages. Drill down until you have a direct path to the connections you want. Find ways to connect to one person at a time, just like in the real world, and build on that. Don't just do what everyone else has done. That's boring (we'll cover the sin of boring later.)

In short, the pathway for direct sellers is, *use what you've already learned about direct selling* and apply it to social media.

The Person-to-Person Future

"Of all things, of all places, perhaps the future of business looks like an Amway convention." ~ Dennis Berman, *Wall Street Journal*

The power and revolution of social media, at its core, is exponential growth and reach. This so close to the same framework of direct selling, it's astonishing.

Imagine, if you will, that in the near future person-to-person selling becomes the primary form of consumer commerce and the favorite method for people to make buying decisions. Imagine that direct selling becomes the principle way to reach consumers. What does that mean for us? For this industry? For your company?

In this future world, what do people shop for? Jewelry perhaps, or health and wellness products, products for their homes, or services like wireless and electricity. Maybe they will ask their social networks about new ways to make money from home.

What if Social Selling is where a significant portion of the $4 trillion in annual US retail sales (Source: *Research And Markets Report 2012*) ends up going in the near future?

What if, to push this a bit further, the actual future of selling depends directly on a model that *rewards people for referrals to their friends?* What if the entire system begins to depend on people referring their friends to specific products, services, and companies, and those companies then deal with their customers personally?

This should sound familiar, as these are things your company is already doing successfully. The industry you've devoted your life to depends on personal selling. So how does that transition into the new business model of Social Selling?

People Trust People They Know—First

Our industry already depends on the idea of trust and referrals, and social media *operates* on a system of referrals. Again, they are mashed up.

SIPRESS

As it stands now, referrals already outweigh advertising for the way modern, connected consumers make purchasing decisions. People trust their social networks more than any other media, or even Google. They depend on advice from their friends and social connections when it comes to making their decisions, and that advice is passed through social media more often than in any other manner. This means that if you're going to enjoy the benefits of personally-referred sales, you also need to be leveraging social media.

In many ways, Amazon and companies like it are quickly coming to dominate the retail world. They represent a kind of "bridge" between traditional media and social media. They're standing with one foot in the old model and one in the new. Social Selling actually improves upon these models.

On Amazon you can read user reviews about everything they sell. But it is still a one-way experience; consumers read a user review, make a purchase, and move on. The consumer is still separated from the company, and has limited social interaction.

Social media – and the idea of Social Selling – takes that connection one step further, because there *is* an interaction. You "follow" someone's reviews on a blog or social platform, and can interact with them daily if you want, by leaving comments and getting responses. You can fully engage and interact with your connections about everything from the best organic products for your baby to the best supplements for good health. Personal connections make for personal recommendations, and that makes for better purchases and consumer experience.

As with any other process, your social news feed may feature a number of updates that don't interest you. But over time you begin to separate (or the social networks separate for you) the wheat from the chaff, the "shills" from the sincere users. You find people who are genuinely there to communicate and interact, rather than sell or promote. You find people who match closely with your personality or your needs, and those who give valuable feedback. Even if someone is selling something, social media is so transparent that to have any kind of success it's almost impossible for them not to be sincere about it.

It's instant, and it's constant, and it's happening all day, every day; whether you're participating or not. Consumers now have real time, constant access to what people are saying or recommending. They can and do ask for advice about their decisions and can summon a crowd's opinion in an instant.

It's no wonder that people are choosing social media over the one-way communication that dominated traditional media and sales for so long. It is just so incredibly *useful* to them. And it will only become more so. Can you even imagine where it will be in five or ten years?

> **"**Consumers now have real time, constant access to what people are saying or recommending. They can and do ask for advice about their decisions and can summon a crowd's opinion in an instant.**"**

As companies and as direct sellers, we have to accept this and adapt to it. As I imparted earlier, the very first thing a person does when they hear about a new opportunity is *check their social networks.* They check their Facebook or Twitter feed to see if anyone else has said anything about this particular company or product. They email or text friends, family, and people they know, asking for feedback. And they'll get a wide array of responses, helping them make an informed decision.

So if they're making decisions in this manner, isn't it absolutely vital that our industry be involved in the conversation? And how can we be involved in the conversation if we aren't a part of the platform?

It's just that simple (and yes, just that complicated). Either way, we know that as direct sellers we've dealt with this before. These are familiar waters; they're just a slightly different shade of blue.

The Decline of Branding (As We Know It)

So now we're looking at a way to connect directly with hundreds, thousands, and maybe even millions of people. We know that these customers all talk to each other. We know that they're using social media for personal recommendations, and that we can start to apply it. Social Selling uses theories that we already practice every day in our industry – personal and professional networking, personal and direct sales, relationships, and follow ups, etc.

So what's not in play here? What's missing from this equation that is supposedly so important in other forms of business?

Brand.

In fact, branding – personal, company, or otherwise – is becoming less and less relevant in relationship-driven commerce. This is another area where we need to adapt to the changing environment.

As much as they have helped us understand what a company or product stands for, brands are not only fading, but in some cases even becoming an encumbrance. In today's society, brands can serve as signs of failing or discredited institutions, and even elicit starkly negative connotations for the companies that promote them. Think BP, Goldman Sachs, and Bank of America. Wal-Mart and McDonalds. These are among the world's largest companies, all suffering underneath their brands.

A quick look at what's happening in activism is quite revealing for brand marketers. People are actually *taking to the streets* – and staying there – to protest *brands!* A tweet or two between friends can become a flash mob, a success story, a celebrity, or even a movement. A message goes out to hundreds and thousands of connections via social media, and becomes a personal call to action.

Suddenly these personal statements become all-important, and reach far beyond brand. This is, in the end, the power of the people and interconnectedness over mighty corporations. In the past few years, entire governments have fallen to their knees in a matter of months by the mechanism of social technology.

What Do We Have That Apple Doesn't?

In my house we are chock full of iPhones, Mac-Books, and iPads. Anyone who knows me will attest to my passion about Apple products. Their products make my life better. I love them. I'm even a (very minor) shareholder.

As much as I admire this company and believe it to be one of the greatest brands ever to grace modern business, there's something Apple doesn't have, and likely will never have. A resource so powerful that Apple sales could have been double or even triple what they have been since introducing the iPhone in 2007.

For everything Apple has, there's one very powerful resource they don't have…

You. Your companies. This business model.

The ability to reach people personally, to motivate them, to inspire them to something better and really improve their lives. Not just with whiz bang gadgetry, *but with real human connection.*

> **"***What if person-to-person compensation for introductions to new products or opportunities was the only selling model that worked anymore?***"**

Apple does not possess *nearly* the personal touch that is represented by you, your colleagues and your field. It does not, cannot, touch real people. Sure millions of people touch (quite literally) its products every day.

In the end, though, Apple is just a brand.

Even the greatest brand we know cannot change lives and reach hearts, *like you can.* Your company can reach people in a way no other industry can.

Imagine what this could mean?

What if person to person compensation for introductions to new products or opportunities was the only selling model that worked anymore?

What if broadcasters, publishers and producers were no longer the recipients of compensation for sales, and that all that money went to people who simply recommended products and services to their friends? What if the old business school mantra of how an advertising impression – leads to recall of a brand – leads to a purchase, was no longer valid?

Social media has changed the world, and personal connections and recommendations are more important than ever. Where does that leave us? Where does that leave our industry?

Simply, this means that *we can be the winners in this new world.* If personal connection becomes the only sales model that *works* … and we're already doing exactly that … then we already know how to do it, and we could ultimately become a primary method of consumer purchasing.

As we've seen by the huge decline in newspapers, TV ads, radio ads, and conventional marketing channels and methods, this is exactly where the world is headed.

The Reinvention of Direct Selling

It's already happening, you know. In fact, it's becoming more and more commonplace to find parts of our direct selling model right there in the mainstream. DirectTV pays people $100 to refer subscribers. Bank of America (again, not the most endearing of companies) will pay you $50 to refer a friend, as will most of their competitors. All of the wireless carriers pay nicely for referrals, and have done so for a while now.

Large companies are coming to realize that people trust their friends and social connections more than advertisements or branding. And they are furiously trying to figure out how to incentivize people to sell for them. Picture hordes of MBA's turning levers and creating pivot tables to exact the golden formula that will lead to personal sales. Direct selling professionals may find that visual amusing. We know the realities.

Referrals are taking over online as well, as we've already seen. Online affiliate marketing networks are one of the fastest growing forms of online commerce on the Internet. People all around the world are setting up little micro-businesses selling other people's products via their websites, and *being paid commissions*. There is a massive online infrastructure to support affiliate selling. Affiliate networks like ClickBank and Commission Junction have centralized the referral economy and created trusted exchanges, where anyone can sell anyone else's products. Amazon, who some say invented the online affiliate model, allows nearly anyone to become a store and get compensated for selling product.

Social First, Selling Second

This *rewards* mentality of mainstream companies is also seeping into our industry. I recently consulted with several new companies who have decided to join our industry because they want to pay out multiple levels of commission. They've figured out that our model scales quickly and represents an interesting new channel for products that might not sell well on a retail shelf.

These new companies want to be "multi-level" in a strict sense of the word, but they reject the idea that a community must be built around their commission plan. "What do we need events for?" they ask me. "Our company story is you'll make money! That's all the story that counts!" They really believe the promise of financial reward alone is enough to recruit, retain, and develop new associates. Kinda cute, isn't it?

Direct sellers like you know that there's a bit more to it than that. It's a naïve, but not uncommon, perspective that monetary reward alone will attract followers. I counsel these folks that there's more to multi-level than just multiple levels of pay. You've got to know how to make people feel important, foster relationships, provide hope and inspiration, and help them develop themselves into better people, if you're going to attract and retain them in your business.

When I explain this to these industry outsiders, their first response is typically a puzzled "Huh?"

Then I tell them, "And above all, you need that Special Something Else…" This of course *really* confuses them.

Direct selling professionals understand these

things intuitively. We know that the "Special Something Else" is what makes our industry unique.

And that's also what's going to help us dominate Social Selling. We understand that the most important thing we do is connect with people, get an understanding of their hopes and dreams, and try to make those dreams come true. It's what's so fun and satisfying about this business, right?

This is where the big guys – the brand names – lose ground. Do chain store retailers make people feel important? Hardly.

> **"***Online sellers hold no events. They don't go on fabulous trips together. They don't get to meet the company founders. They never walk across a stage. They don't make friends and have fun like we do.***"**

Does Ebay foster relationships? Actually, yes – it's called the "dispute resolution process."

Can people truly enhance their lives through solitary affiliate selling? Now that is *laughable*.

Online sellers hold no events. They don't go on

fabulous trips together. They don't get to meet the company founders. They never walk across a stage.

They don't make friends and have fun like we do.

It's a lonely business, selling things online. It's difficult to leverage personal connections, and it's almost impossible to offer non-monetary yet psychologically satisfying incentives.

So there is an enormous – and growing – void between the brand-driven sales of the old days and the current vast wasteland of impersonal online selling. This is where we come in!

We have that Special Something, and we know how to use it. We have the breadth of innovative offerings, the infrastructure, and the deep understanding, ingrained over a hundred years, of how to motivate and reward people.

We can do it better than anyone else, we've built an entire industry around it. We like people. We *get* people. And that's what's important about Social Selling. It's all about the people, and understanding how to connect with them.

If we do this right, our industry will make possible an entire world of person-to-person commerce, far beyond the perceived limits of today.

But for that to happen, first we need to get a handle on some things:

We need to accept that the world is definitely moving in this direction.

We need to acknowledge that the direction is headed right for our areas of expertise.

We need to act on this knowledge, rather than wait around while mainstream companies and affiliate networks encroach on our turf.

We need to *own* it, because let's face it – person-to-person selling is *our* world!

Now is the time to act.

Chapter 3

Social Selling Strategies

"And that is how change happens. One gesture. One person. One moment at a time."~ Libba Bray, The Sweet Far Thing

HOPEFULLY YOU'RE NO LONGER ON THE fence about the importance of social media for your company's and this industry's future.

So how can you maximize the wealth of growth potential silently lurking in your company's Twitter, Facebook, or LinkedIn accounts? How can you capitalize on the energy, vitality and immediacy of Social Selling?

What you need is a strategy– one that is specific and unique to you and your company; a proven, efficient way to put your talents, time, and energy into action.

The Power of the Personal Touch

More than just words, quotes, statistics, inspiration, or motivation, a Social Selling strategy gives you power, and translates your thoughts and plans into action.

Very important to our industry, essential really, is that Social Selling allows us to maintain the personal one-on-one relationships that make what we do so unique. It allows us to enhance the personal touches our model depends on, while reaching more people than we ever conceived of a short ten years ago.

But we have to do it the right way if it's going to work. One thing I urge against in the field of social media practices is the generic, static, me-too social media campaigns that tend to dominate our industry and others.

Browse through the major social media sites and it's about dialogue – imagery, stories, information, education, entertainment, humor, quips, witticism, personality, and personal creativity.

Me-too, generic campaigns miss the point about personal touch. In losing that, they lose the value of the social media. The answer, then, is to go out of your way to be as personal and real as possible. Use your company's personality and individuality to make stronger, more unique, and lasting personal connections. Allow your company to show its true colors, there where everyone can see you. Show what makes you accessible and unique. And those things lead to people thinking of you as human, and learning to trust you.

With a strong Social Selling strategy, you can

reach people's timelines anytime without bothering the people themselves. You can work passively, politely, in your own style. What's more, you can do as little as "poke" them, or you can share something interesting, praise, and even thank them.

> **❝**Words of encouragement are the currency of our business, and social media is Fort Knox.**❞**

The opportunity to touch people, reach out and recognize or praise them, is directly in line with what we do in this industry. Words of encouragement are the currency of our business, and social media is Fort Knox.

Start where you're comfortable. First, look at the media and build your own plan. Find a way for it to work within your comfort zone. If you can start there, and accept the "gift" of what Social Selling platforms can do for you, then you can move and grow as your comfort increases. In the end, the possibilities are endless—for reaching out to individuals and people, connecting with them, and guiding their decisions.

Premier Designs: Keeping it Personal

One example of a company who successfully made the transition is Premier Designs.

Founded in 2001, the jewelry company is widely known for its positive, inspirational culture and the endearment of its original founders, Joan and Andy Horner. The company prides itself on one-to-one relationships and an incredibly supportive environment for its field, including a company-sponsored phone support line and the personal involvement of the corporate team in the success of its Jewelers. The company has built a supportive community that today is the envy of the industry.

A cornerstone of Premier's culture is the oft-repeated mantra "keep it personal." The company vowed years ago not to "go online" or take on the fad technologies of the day. It has especially eschewed technologies such as ecommerce that appeared to diminish the relationships inherent in its field, no matter how more efficient or profitable "selling product" could become. The company views its Jewelers, not the products themselves, to be the most important part of the company.

One can imagine the move to social media for a company like this would appear a difficult one for the company to commit to. As company President Tim Horner describes, "We felt social media by its nature of being 'easy,' could diminish the connections between our Jew-

elers and weaken the bonds that are so important to who we are."

Yet, after several years of watching from the sidelines and listening to its Jewelers, the company decided to cautiously enter the often rapidly changing and fast-moving world of social media.

"Once we learned the power of social media to enhance, rather than replace, those relationships, we began to get excited about the possibilities to do even more to connect and support our people. More importantly, we found our field was already on social media and were eager to connect with us there. We haven't looked back since."

In November 2011, as a result of careful planning as well as the day-to-day involvement of executives from different departments, Premier Designs enjoyed one of the most successful social media launches in industry history. Their success continues on today with a vibrant and robust social media presence that brings people into their community, and of course, keeps it all personal.

Where Conversation Is Happening

So, to begin our discussion about strategy, let's start with a place. Where is everybody hanging out these days? Where should your company focus its resources? To begin composing your Social Selling road map, you need a simple visual of where conversations are happening.

Message Boards, Photo, Sharing, Widgets, Videos, Social Networks, Forums, and Blogs are just a few of the spaces online where conversations are taking place.

These activities are all powered by a dizzying array of social media tools available to anyone for free. Most are quite easy to use. Tools like:

Facebook	Hulu	slideshare
Twitter	Vimeo	foursquare
Pinterest	cafemom	Badoo
LinkedIn	DailyMotion	Posterous
YouTube	Squidoo	Bit.ly
Wordpress	Fanpop	About.me
Blogger	epinions	Picasa
Photobucket	Digg	Scribd
Flickr	StumbleUpon	Merchant Circle
Wordpress	UStream	blogger
MySpace	Kaboodle	instagram
Flickr	reddit	and so on
photobucket	delicious	

...and many others yet to be launched. The entrepreneurial site killerstartup.com says each day it reviews fifteen newly-launched website ventures, most having a primary social networking component.

Day by day, Social Selling becomes not only more powerful but more ubiquitous and universal.

Your strategy will dictate what kinds of tools you will leverage. For example, companies who view social media as an ongoing core function of the company (and they should) may choose tools like Facebook and Twitter that build their community over time. Other companies more focused on driving short term revenue may put more of their resources into email and online marketing tools like Google Adwords (yes there are niche strategies for using online ads for direct selling).

Once you know the strategy you can set your sights on the core platforms for your Social Selling plan.

It's All About Momentum

From here, we start to put what we've learned in our own industry into play. As we all know, direct selling is not like other industries. Our online communities are very different than those of, say, an online supplement company. We already thrive on networks of real life fans, and followers. We focus on satisfying our distributors' unique wants and needs.

While other industries can live on occasional, superficial interaction with their platform, direct sellers must keep the excitement going 24/7. Momentum is critical in our industry, both online and off. And when it works, one feeds the other.

For our needs, less really is more. Rather than leap in and start "grabbing names" with the wrongheaded assumption that more is more, focus instead on growing naturally in ways that are going to be meaningful and sincere to your existing and future networks.

Be Fun or Be Done

"If you're not having fun, you're doing
something wrong."
~ Groucho Marx

It's important for your social sites to be fun. It takes creativity (more than you'll sometimes be able to muster) coupled with connectivity. Painting a picture is creative, but not necessarily connective. Social media on the other hand is *interactive* expression. Many might say the immediate response it can elicit is a true paradise for artists who crave feedback. Most people just like the attention and the ability to reach people with their message.

We are in the business we're in because we love people – connecting with them, working with them, sharing with them, and selling with them. So think of this as a social experience, rather than work.

> **"**The people who follow you and read your posts expect to be entertained, and you can't let them down.**"**

There's another, more important reason to make your Social Selling exploits fun – your field expects it. Like it or not, today's corporations – especially in direct selling – are in demand to serve as providers of information, community and entertainment as much as products or services. Your online networks – the people who follow you and read your posts – expect to be entertained, and you can't let them down. Fun is the driving force behind many of the fastest growing direct sellers today.

The most progressive direct sellers today are laser focused on the "relationship experience" with their field. Companies like Mary Kay, AdvoCare and Premier Designs, for example, have created brands and personalities that demonstrate fun and a sense of belonging. These are relationships that people want to be part of.

We are in the lifestyle business. By lifestyle, I don't mean the "you too can have this car!" lifestyle; I mean a place for people to belong and feel a part of something bigger than themselves. A place to learn and grow and, yes, add to income. Be fun and entertaining and even a bit goofy, as you lead them to something bigger.

Fun is a primary driver for recruitment and retention, and if you don't figure out how to build this culture you will be forever stuck in churn-land, having to rebuild your business once or even twice a year. And that's not much fun.

Get into a couple of social media platforms and start building your network. Be selective, and add people who will improve your network and be interested in what you have to say. Then start learning how to post updates that are fun and entertaining. The more entertaining you are, the more likely they are to stick around, and tell their friends about you.

What to Avoid in Your Social Selling Strategy

Sometimes it can be as helpful to learn what not to do as well as what to do. It gives us some starting boundaries. Here are a few helpful tips in that regard.

1. **Don't be boring.** You are not boring. You couldn't have made it this far in the industry if you were. So in the relaxed, un-self-conscious way to which you are accustomed, flourish in your company's quirks and eccentricities, even poke fun at your own character flaws (we all have 'em). Being boring online may be worse than not being online at all. Repeating yourself, posting things nobody cares about, not posting

enough, posting all the time, not leveraging videos or pictures, and just plain being uninteresting are all boring. Our industry is notorious for repetitive posts and updates about this event or that promotion. Ban it! It kills your interactivity.

Don't poop on your Facebook community.

Sometimes smothering a page's interactivity happens by accident.

One of our more recent social media management clients was having trouble with their company pre-enrollment site in advance of their company launch.

As interest in the company climbed, some in the field complained the corporate web site was competitive to the distributor replicated sites. To resolve this, a decision was made by the home office to put a notice on the corporate web page instructing people to visit the company's Facebook page to "identify a distributor to sign up under." (No, we were not consulted in advance.)

Can you guess what happened next? The Facebook page was inundated with pitches, replicated sites links and promotions trying to get the attention of new visitors looking for a sponsor. Unfortunately the majority of the page Likers clicked off and stopped interacting with the page, and the page's analytics showed a steep drop off not only in interactivity and excitement, but in new Likers. No one wants to walk into a room of frenzied salespeople.

The situation was corrected quickly, but not without a hard lesson. Online communities are delicate and anything that effects yin and yang of your fans and followers should be considered carefully.

2. **Avoid selling.** People use social media to share, learn and have fun. They are not there to buy things (this is why it's taken Facebook ads awhile to catch on). This doesn't mean they won't buy, at least eventually, but that's not why they log in. Constant shouts about your latest promotion or event will turn away many otherwise eager fans. Remember, social comes before selling for a reason. Until last year, we recommended that eighty percent of our clients' posts and updates be about things other than themselves or their products. They were free to post about their business twenty percent of the time (note I didn't say "sell"). Now, with the increase in noise and clogged newsfeeds, we keep to a strict 90/10 rule. Only ten percent of your posts should be self-interested *at all*.

3. **Avoid being unsubscribed.** Just as people can "Like" your company on Facebook, they can also "unsubscribe" to it. And you'll never even know it. Unsubscribing is polite. And clean. With one click your Liker won't see your updates anymore. They haven't rejected you, they just reject every single thing you say. They will still appear as a

fan of your company. Before you post or update the page's status, ask yourself, "Will this annoy people enough to unsubscribe?" If the answer is anything even close to a maybe, rework it or don't post it at all.

4. **Avoid having the wrong people at the controls.** Hire an expert with deep knowledge of both direct selling *and* social media (the combination of the two is the essence of Social Selling), and make sure they understand how they go together. Although our firm does a lot of this work, it doesn't have to be hired out. There are several examples of companies who do social media well internally; the daunting part is finding the right person who is affordable who also has strong knowledge in both areas. If the role is internal, the person should be full time and devoted exclusively to building community, connection and content.

5. **Avoid a "net casting" approach.** Stop trying to get dates and start making relationships happen. This takes patience, commitment and class, both offline and on. Make what you do online fun, but also make in interesting and most importantly, make it last.

Chapter 4

The Tools of Social Selling

"We have technology, finally, that for the first time in human history allows people to really maintain rich connections with much larger numbers of people." ~ Pierre Omidyar, eBay Founder

ALRIGHT, SO NOW YOU HAVE A plan, a number of strategies at your disposal, and you should have a picture in your head of a world filled with social media. You're starting to see how this is a natural step for anyone in the direct selling industry. Now you must get comfortable with it.

In this chapter, we focus on some of the sites well-suited for direct sellers. Some sites and tools not covered here, such as Google Plus, photo sharing sites like Flickr and social bookmarking sites like Digg are important as well and should also be considered as a part of your social marketing mix.

Social Networking – The Analog Version

When we hold our project kickoff meetings with clients, one of the things that helps put social media in perspective is during the educational portion of our meeting is to imagine each social network as it might be in the real world. All social networks have an "analog" (or real world) version of themselves.

The Facebook Barbeque

When it comes to social media, no site is more popular or widely used than Facebook. I would add statistics here for you but it would make this book obsolete in a month. Let's just say Facebook boasts more than a billion users. *One billion.*

What makes Facebook so special? What took it from Mark Zuckerberg's original "Facemash" site at Harvard to one of the most valuable companies in the world in less than ten years? What created this cultural phenomenon?

The secret is more psychological than technological.

Facebook works extremely hard at capturing the very complicated dynamics of human relationships into digital form. This is no small achievement. In Facebook, you can introduce yourself or re-meet people (friend them), send a "thinking about you" card (poke them), or smile at something they say (Like a comment). You can decide who sees you and who doesn't. You can also choose to not care about

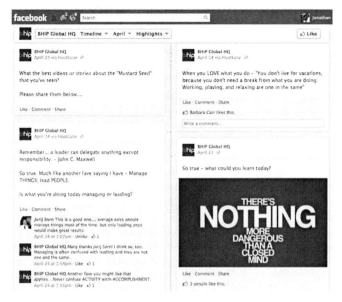

Sample Facebook page: bHIP Global's page is a daily source of inspirational quotes and interaction.

their interests (unsubscribe) or even turn your back on them (un-friend.)

Just like in the real world.

Facebook's expertise into the human experience obviously goes far deeper than I could list here, even if I knew how they did it. It's unreal sometimes, the similarities. I dare say it's...human, in a way. And yes, a little creepy.

So what's the analog, real world parallel to Facebook? I like to call it the "backyard barbeque" of social networking. If you put on a barbeque event at your home, who might show up? A neighbor, a close

Sample posts from the Momofactor Facebook Page

friend, someone you knew in high school. Even your boss might stop by. They're all there, virtually. It's a gathering place, friendly, casual, relaxed.

By being at your home your guests learn about you,

your personal likes and dislikes, interest and hobbies. They see photos of your family. Most of all they laugh, share, talk about sports, the weather, what's in the news or movies. You know, backyard banter.

What's not happening at the Facebook barbeque? Think anyone might show up with a table and start trying to sell products? Or keep repeating themselves again and again about a special event that will change your life? Not likely. If it got too loud or full of salespeople, most would mumble something about an early work day and scoot their boots out of there.

A few words about what Facebook is, followed by what it isn't.

Ten Things Facebook *is*	Ten Things Facebook *isn't*
1. A gathering place for like-minded people	1. A megaphone
2. A place to interact in a lively conversation	2. A postcard
3. A "melting pot" of professional and personal views	3. A business card
4. A chance to hear directly from prospects	4. A personal website
5. A transparent opportunity to engage your target audience	5. A lecture
6. A discussion	6. A speech
7. A conversation	7. A rant

8. An opportunity	8. An advertisement
9. A place to form lasting connections that matter	9. An obligation
10. A powerful, passionate, purposeful gathering place	10. A lottery ticket

Tips to Increase Your Facebook Success and Be Seen

So you've spent a good hour perfecting a funny post in the hopes it goes viral. You polish it up one last time, hit "share," and then ... nothing. No comments or shares or even "likes." No one "likes" it!

Don't worry, it's not you (well, not *all* you.) Posting something to your people doesn't guarantee that they'll ever see it, even if it was right up their alley. This is primarily because Facebook's software establishes relevancy, person by person, to each and everything you do, and only shows people what it deems interesting to them.

Facebook's "Boring Filter"

As a user, Facebook's filtering of content is a good thing. To keep your news feed relevant, Facebook's algorithm (known as "EdgeRank") hides boring content for you.

If your engagement behavior shows that you're not interested in your aunt or her cats, for example, then your aunt's constant posts about her kitties may be less likely to display on your newsfeed. You don't need to do a thing. Facebook does it for you. You never see the kitties, and have Edgerank to thank for it.

In the same vein, if you have pseudo-friends you have never interacted with, they are less likely to show in your feed, Facebook deems them less relevant to you. Conversely, those whose profiles you've read, traded messages or wall posts with, or newly added will show up more often. (See how your activity affects your visibility?)

Similar to how Google ranking works, Facebook's algorithm ranks the importance of certain content, albeit with very different parameters.

> **"***If you have pseudo-friends you have never interacted with, they are less likely to show in your feed, Facebook deems them less relevant to you.***"**

For companies, who in most cases will not command the majority of a viewer's interest, it is even more difficult to be noticed. In fact, most business pages rank lower than friend pages. Moontoast. com says 70% of fans post once to a business page and *never* return. And more than ninety percent of fans never return to the page they've just "liked."

What this tells us is that most fans engage with your content through their own news feed, NOT the fan page. This makes ranking even more important.

The truth is a majority of Facebook posts today are never seen in news feeds. Even this seemingly straightforward area of the Internet is governed by laws of supply and demand. It's crowded out there – with a billion users at an average of 175 friends each, the chances of your posts being noticed on Facebook (much less shared) diminish every day.

Edgerank looks at what is called an "affinity score" (how often the user interacts with the page), "weight" (how many comments and tags, etc. a post has), and

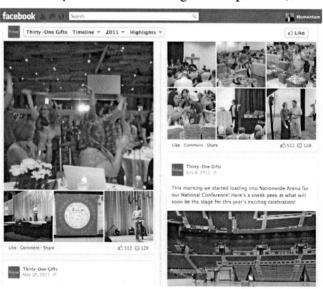

Sample Facebook page: Thirty-One Gifts show their excitement.

time decay. The answer helps determine what shows on whose feeds for how long.

Underneath all this is an extremely fast and sophisticated algorithm that reconciles your profile with those of your friends. Because the feed is so crowded now, in many cases your post may have only a few minutes or even seconds in someone else's feed before it's replaced with something else.

This has caused panic in marketing circles because, of course, *you can't engage people who cannot be reached.* You could have the most creative, spontaneous content on earth, but unless a tipping point of people see and share it, it goes nowhere.

What makes the difference? Interesting content that gets shared, consistently.

Three Steps to Getting Noticed

But before you give up and go digging in your pocket for ad money, let's look at how your posts go beyond your homepage and into the timeline to get noticed by other people. How will you stand out? Here are a few tips:

Step 1: Interact Strategically

Each time you interact on Facebook you add to your EdgeRank profile. The best approach to increasing your posts' exposure is to interact with them manually and consistently.

Select the people and pages you want in your circle, and comment, post, and tag them consistently.

Converse with their friends on a regular basis. This can help put you in the conversation, and hopefully on your targets' feeds.

Tags weigh heavily. Tag the people in photos and posts who matter to you. (Don't tag popular people just to ride coat tails, it isn't very effective and can get you "de-friended".)

Step 2: Pay Attention to Timing

Remember, "decay" is a major factor in how long your post remains in news feeds. If most of your friends are social drinkers, posting a business story on Friday night is probably not an effective strategy. By the time they check, it's probably been awhile since you posted, and they may be too hung-over to care. That means your post is decaying before they check for it; in that case, there's a good chance that it's already out of the newsfeed.

In direct selling (where every hour is a business hour), I find posting on weekends to be pretty effective, as many people seem to take a little extra time to update status and check their newsfeed. Mondays are awful days to post, in my experience, as people are geared for work and glancing through at best.

Step 3: Make it Easy to "Like" You

We like people in real life for the same reasons we like them on Facebook. Smart, courteous, interesting, and funny people are generally likeable. People who enjoy listening to themselves talk all day are less likeable. Brush up on your Dale Carnegie if you need a refresher in what it takes to be liked – the old man's wisdom still applies, even in social media.

The number of posts you create is important and should be dependent on the number of Likes the page has. A page with a few hundred Likes should post less frequently, a few thousand likes means more frequent posting. Better to post more than less, because a post not made is definitely not seen. But try not to overdo it – you don't want to be that guy or gal at the barbeque who just won't shut up.

Interact, a lot. Comment on posts, share, and tag people. And make sure that all your web properties are integrated with Facebook so people can Like and share away from your page.

Sample Google+ page: ACN making good use of video.

The Twitter Cocktail Party

One of the more common things I hear at our client training sessions is "Fine, I can do Facebook, but I just don't get Twitter." Sometimes asking busy executives to begin tweeting gets the same response my ten-year-old gives when asked her to clean her room: *"Do I have to?"* Of course not, but who wants to live in messy room all the time? (Ok, wrong metaphor, but you get the picture.)

" We've just joined the tweetering classes."

As you begin interacting with others through social media in earnest, you might find yourself falling into one of two camps: Facebook or Twitter. While there's always room for both, people tend to work with what works best for them. They simply gravitate to where they feel most comfortable.

For some, that will be the orderly, private (I use that term lightly) nature of Facebook. For others, it will be the fast-pace and vast openness of Twitter. It pays to explore all the tools, each has its own purpose and best use for business.

One of the unique features of Twitter is its simplicity. There are only really 4 or 5 core functions to learn. Its profile pictures are small, the backgrounds are static, the feeds are fast, and the messages are clear and efficient (of course, @some r not so #clear).

Officially, tweeted messages are limited to 140 characters; in practice it's only 120, to allow space for "re-tweets" and replies.

While Facebook users can post pictures and links and long passages at will, Twitter keeps things relatively low-tech. Perhaps that's one of the reasons behind its popularity.

What's tough about Twitter is its relatively steep learning curve. How it works is not obvious to the uninitiated. So people set up a profile, get confused immediately and never go back to that source of humiliation again.

Those who stick with it are treated to an amazing world of information on any topic, shared with

33 Jonathan Gilliam @MomoFactor   12 May
The Do's and Don'ts for Marketing With Pinterest
entrepreneur.com/article/223489 via @entmagazine
Expand

33 Jonathan Gilliam @MomoFactor   12 May
RT @mashsocialmedia How well do you know the most important
facts in Facebook's IPO filing? on.mash.to/KOsyaY
Expand

33 Jonathan Gilliam @MomoFactor   12 May
@marketerexpo Thanks for the mention. This is truly appreciated.
💬 View conversation

33 Jonathan Gilliam @MomoFactor   12 May
@jillney You're most welcome! Have a great day!
💬 View conversation

33 Jonathan Gilliam @MomoFactor   12 May
Begin this beautiful weekend with a happy heart and big smile. Good
morning! #greetings
Expand

33 Jonathan Gilliam @MomoFactor   11 May
Just caught Beachbody president Jonathan Gelfand on the CBS
Evening News in a story about counterfeiting, a big...
fb.me/23kLRh863
Expand   ← Reply   🗑 Delete   ★ Favorite

33 Jonathan Gilliam @MomoFactor   11 May
Rep update: Google Algorithm Change Causes SEO/ORM Panic
j.mp/K6IlRf #SEO #ORM
Expand

Sample tweets from the @Momofactor Twitter page.

few filters, instantly, worldwide. That feature alone is
what brings forty-year dictatorships to their knees.
And yes, it's fine for talking about the cheese sand-
wich you just ate, if that's what you're into. It's truly
Live.

> **"***Those who stick to learning Twitter are treated to an amazing world of information on any topic, shared with few filters, instantly, worldwide.***"**

For direct sellers, Twitter's low-key approach can be a real boon. You can "tweet" short messages as often as you like, and "follow" people who belong to the categories you're most interested in connecting with. You can reply to people who make interesting comments, and even take things private with Direct Messages. It's quicker and more succinct than Facebook, and you have the option of interacting with a much larger group of people. You can connect with people much more easily than on Facebook – it's much easier to find groups and networks on this platform.

Twitter can also feel like a release valve compared with Facebook. You can post more often about whatever you like and not be punished for it as you might on Facebook. "Finally I can really communicate with the field and not get unsubscribed!" you may say.

However, being interesting and interactive is just as important on Twitter as on Facebook. It's just different. If all you do on Twitter is talk about your product or company, people won't follow you or see your updates, same as Facebook.

Your goal on Twitter is to share interesting things, opinions, interests and humor to build a following that you can eventually build trust with. It's sort of like being at a cocktail party. What do you do there? You mingle, you chat. (Yes you might drink, but that's not recommended when tweeting!) You might meet a stranger who happens to share the same interests as you.

What, again, is not a part of cocktail mingling? Any tables filled with brochures? Shouting salespeople? Nope, you passed them at the "follow" button.

Maximize Twitter for Direct Selling

There are huge benefits to Twitter for direct selling companies. You can share lots of news and information related to the business. Anything urgent can be shared and you can be confident it will be picked up by the field instantly and further shared. Think of the promotional value here, the buzz-building, all the announcements. The free-wheeling, informal conversation you can have with your field, directly.

I recall being first captivated by Twitter while attending a professional conference sometime after Twitter was launched. I found that via "live Tweeting," people were able to chat about the presenters and their topics —*while the presentation was happening.* Like an invisible chat room in real time, the audience would often take a snippet or blurb from the presenter and tweet it out to room, their following and the world. Or they might disagree with something a speaker was saying—while they were saying it! I thought that was the coolest thing ever, and I had to learn it.

When I speak on stage these days I am ever aware that people may be live tweeting about me, so I need to be smart and funny and interesting. It raises my game. People could throw virtual tomatoes at me, but who cares? It's interactive, and that's the neat part! If I'm on a panel and not speaking, often I will be on Twitter—from the stage, "in the stream" and responding to comments in real time. So cool.

Think this might be a great tool for your field to use at your events? I've got news for you — they already are. I see tweets all the time from people attending direct selling conventions and meetings. Another reason to get into the conversation.

Ten things Twitter *is*	Ten things Twitter *isn't*
1. An opportunity to speak your mind in 140 characters or less	1. A megaphone
2. A place to engage, interact, and communicate	2. A postcard
3. A portal for open-minded communication	3. A business card

4. A great place to begin active discussions	4. A personal website
5. A place where every word counts	5. A lecture
6. A discussion starter	6. A speech
7. A conversation piece	7. A rant
8. An opportunity to connect instantly	8. An advertisement
9. A place where words matter and thoughts rule	9. An obligation
10. A powerful, passionate, purposeful gathering place	10. A lottery ticket

Social Media Recognition: The Holy Grail for Direct Sellers

With all these benefits to direct sellers, in my opinion one of the most compelling uses of Twitter, all the social platforms really, is the ability to reach out directly to the field *and pat them on the back.*

The power of social media to recognize accomplishment and reward people is severely underestimated—and underutilized—by our industry. Yet it is one of the most powerful and perfect aspects of Social Selling. And it doesn't cost a penny. No stage to build, not even a postage stamp to lick. Just a few kind words typed in a box.

And it *works.* People can be lonely online. They may be saying things they find amusing or profound, yet it sometimes seems as if no one cares what they say. Maybe the newsfeed is edging them out, or they just don't know how to use it correctly. Think a personal, public reply to them on Twitter from the company CEO might make a difference in this person's day? Heck yeah!

I'm getting excited just typing these words. I'll say it here: *The power to recognize and appreciate our people on social media may be the very best thing about Social Selling.* This is what we DO for a living.

Anatomy of a Direct Selling Tweet

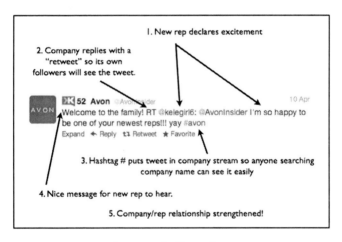

Anatomy of a Tweet: Avon

At the very least, aside from the human voice, social media has shown the highest cost/effectiveness ratio of any recognition tool our industry has ever used.

The LinkedIn Trade Show

Unlike Facebook and Twitter, which are social media sites in the strictest sense of the word, LinkedIn is a professionally oriented platform, and may be just the kickoff site you need for dipping your toe into the social media waters.

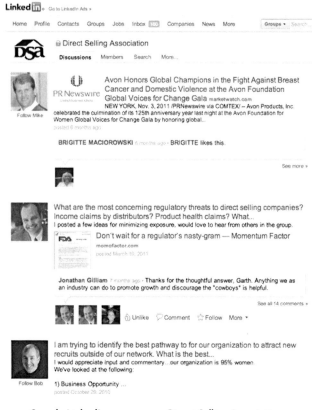

Sample LinkedIn group page: Direct Selling Association

LinkedIn, the world's number two social site, was started and continues to evolve as a premiere business networking site. I often describe LinkedIn's "real world analog" as a professional conference or trade show. Folks are more conservative, they're professional, they're trading business information and networking. They might be selling something (many indeed are) but few are shouting. Instead they are connecting and putting people together. Presenting and sharing, rather than promoting.

How to Start on LinkedIn as an Individual

While some new users will hop on LinkedIn and "grab" as many connections as they can right away, this is the online equivalent of collecting business cards at a networking event. Not very interactive.

Instead, you'll want to take your time with this platform. Start by setting up a thorough, professional, and specific profile, before connecting with anyone. Know what you're there for and build your profile accordingly. Use a professional profile picture, add the dates, businesses, and contacts from your resume, and follow the steps to have a complete and attractive profile.

Next, begin connecting with friends you already know. Use the handy "search" box or email contact uploader function to connect with people you work with. When you find colleagues, friends, family, and coworkers, send them an invitation to connect.

On LinkedIn you are instantly qualified. If someone accepts your invitation, you have an opening to connect further – and you should. Write them a personal greeting or message, thanking them for the connection.

As you begin to connect on LinkedIn, use it like you would use the other social platforms, and start to interact. Spend time on the site, navigate it carefully, and learn how to use it. Write and request "recommendations." Join groups (the DSA has a wonderful LinkedIn group for its members.) As with all these sites, it may take some time to "get up to speed" before you feel comfortable there or can navigate it successfully. Test out the bells and whistles, kick the tires, and stick around.

Like many industries (especially ours) people learn about deals and opportunities through social contact. Those contacts happen much quicker on LinkedIn than in the real world. You can "get to" an important contact through mutual connections, far faster than you could in real life, if ever.

What's interesting about LinkedIn for Social Selling is, of all the social networks, this is the one where people are actively looking for opportunities. How does this intersect with direct sellers? First and foremost, anyone looking for a new job is there. People looking to make additional income may be there as well. It is easy to strike up a conversation about business and entrepreneurialism on LinkedIn; there are many, many small business owners and entrepreneurs from around the world who use it daily.

Given the above, for some reason direct selling companies have been slow to leverage LinkedIn. I suspect it's because they don't really understand how to make it work for their field. But of course that doesn't mean the field hasn't already taken it on. They use it all the time.

There's no doubt there is a match of LinkedIn and Social Selling. We as an industry need to leverage the availability of the millions on LinkedIn who seek connections and opportunity.

Say Yes to YouTube

Most direct sellers have already discovered YouTube and are using it in a big way. The field especially loves YouTube because it's free, easy to use and incredibly sharable. Everyone interacts with YouTube in some way. Surprisingly, it is the number two search engine in the world, behind Google (which of course makes it number one since Google owns it.)

As much as we utilize YouTube to search or host our video, YouTube is in essence a social site and can be a real game-changer. It is difficult to fit here all the ways to leverage YouTube; however it won't take long for you to find great examples of direct sellers who are quite prolific with it. There are countless applications for us using video.

Just perusing my YouTube channel, I found some nice examples of industry YouTube-ery:

- A beautiful video from Rodan + Fields about their next incentive trip resort destination
- A Thanksgiving dessert video from Dove Chocolate Discoveries
- A video of the latest line of fashion jewelry from Bamboopink

Nice YouTube-ery: Stream Energy Chairman Rob Snyder's trademark soccer kick at their convention.

- A weight loss video from Yoli
- A documentary-style video from LIMU about the science behind their products
- A compensation plan training video from bHIP Global
- A corporate introductory video from Regal Ware
- A behind the scenes photo shoot from Sabika Jewelry
- A five-minute tutorial on applying makeup from Mary Kay
- A seven-minute workout video from Beachbody

The industry has certainly embraced the use of video to tell stories and engage people. This is a wonderful thing. Because with video, the possibilities are endless.

There are several other platforms and tools for video, and many companies tend to gravitate to hosting video on their own sites. We advise our clients to stick with YouTube due to its inherent sharing and search power. The fact that it's free doesn't hurt either. The more who see your video and interact with it, the better. On YouTube, people can comment and share, and you can to respond to them, giving it social interaction as well (YouTube comments, thankfully, can be moderated and controlled.)

YouTube is not just for broadcasting your content; it's for interacting.

One of the best things about the rise of YouTube is

that the need for large scale production investments to tell your story has all but disappeared. Companies been have built with video on nothing more than a Flipcam. The general public does not expect or even necessarily prefer to watch highly polished or produced videos anymore. What's most important is what's on the inside, the content. What's being said? Is it genuine and authentic? Or does it feel too polished?

People today have what I've called (publicly— I know, I shouldn't) very sensitive "bullshit meters". When they watch any corporate video they are on the lookout for anything that seems ma-

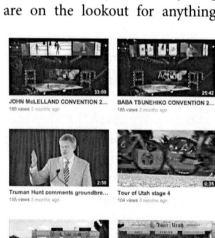

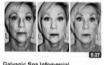

JOHN McLELLAND CONVENTION 2...	BABA TSUNEHIKO CONVENTION 2...	Galvanic Spa Infomercial
188 views 2 months ago	185 views 2 months ago	9,817 views 5 months ago
Truman Hunt comments groundbre...	Tour of Utah stage 4	Tour of Utah Stage 3
155 views 5 months ago	104 views 5 months ago	81 views 5 months ago
Tour of Utah stage 2	Tour of Utah Final stage	GroundBreaking
55 views 5 months ago	35 views 5 months ago	27 views 5 months ago

Sample YouTube page: NuSkin utilizes video in multiple ways.

nipulative or forced. The best thing you can do with the video you produce is *make sure it's as real as it can be.* By its very definition, overly produced and airbrushed videos with models and actors and smiles all around, are just not real.

YouTube is of course, useful as a social network, too. Rather than simply making videos and uploading them, view other videos in your areas of interest and interact with the posters. Leave observations about their videos, ask questions to get them talking.

The point is to keep it fluid, not static. While videos themselves are great, making one and posting it and then leaving it there to gather virtual dust is no different than writing a blog post and never following up on any of the reader comments. The important part is introducing the material and then using it to build connections with people of your choice.

Precision With Pinterest

A recent addition to the Social Selling lineup, Pinterest may be the perfect social media site for the industry in some ways. Pinterest is an online pinboard where users can organize things they love and share them.

Launched in 2010, Pinterest boasts millions of monthly visitors, and is the fastest-growing social networking site today. It's a big hit with women — 70 per cent of users are female, matching our industry demographic perfectly.

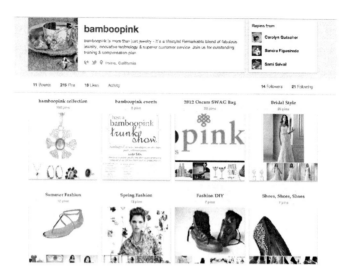

Example of Pinterest Pinboard: Bamboopink

For that reason, we recommend that our clients in party plan, product-focused, or "theme" companies (such as eco-friendly or fashion-based) absolutely embrace Pinterest. In fact, if your company does anything interesting at all — and I hope it does — it should consider building a Pinterest presence.

Different from Facebook, Pinterest develops a social network through interests and ideas first rather than through people; it first builds connections between interests and shares them with others.

> **"**Pinterest is a big hit with women — 70 per cent of users are female, matching our industry demographic perfectly.**"**

With Pinterest, you can follow others, and others can follow you, somewhat similar to Twitter, allowing you to create a more expansive circle with whom to converse and share. But unlike other social media, it focuses primarily on visual appeal, pins of videos and pictures being the primary eye catchers. It's the shared interests that create the common frame of reference between "pinners".

Here's how to help your company get started with a Pinterest strategy:

1. Support your field with great content

It's important that the home office stays involved and provides "pinnable" information to help associates position themselves as the "go to" person for these products in their community or circle of friends. This starts with quality photos. Great content provided by corporate for any social network helps the field with your message and reduce the need for them to create it themselves. Pinterest provides a "no brainer" way to share company created information, graphics and photos.

2. Create boards that show what your company is about

Though you may be inclined to start promoting your brand in Pinterest by pinning boards filled with your products, it's important to remember that this is still a social networking site that helps you connect and engage with your audience. It's far better to build followers first by creating boards that show what your company is about and what its members are passionate about.

By doing this, you can show off the personality behind your brand and make your company more personable and likable.

3. Start creating boards that include occasional photos of your products

Once you get the hang of Pinterest and have acquired a good following, you can start creating boards that include photos of your products. Remember not to fill one board with all of your products though – that would scream self-promotion and may not sit well with your followers. Instead, feature other visual content that relates to your products.

For example, if you're selling makeup, you can include pictures of women wearing makeup in different situations, such as the right look for a night about town or a job interview. It helps your followers visualize how they can use your products effectively and it adds to your pinboard's visual appeal.

4. Host contests on Pinterest

You conduct interactive and fun contests for your company, why not host one on Pinterest? You can ask your audience and followers to create a pinboard on their account that shows why they like your products or how they use your products in their daily lives. You can be the judge of who the winner is, or you can even ask your other followers to vote for the best board.

This is an excellent way to create buzz around your brand and increase brand awareness. Some creative ways include a hostess who posts a new shipment or award she's received; the company can then provide a drawing for another prize for everyone who does that; or asking a product picture to be repinned and then a prize awarded from a drawing of everyone who repinned an item.

5. Discover what your audience loves

By viewing your customers' and fields' pinboards, you can gain insight on what they love and what they're passionate about. This can help you in your marketing strategy, since it's all about discovering what your customers want and need.

6. Use Pinterest to drive traffic to your website

The whole idea is to spark up interest—*pin*terest—

in your company and its products. You'll want to use links that direct to your site or your field's replicated sites to measure your campaigns.

As a direct seller, Pinterest provides a great platform where people can get to know you, from customers to your leaders and field in general. Set up boards for your executives' favorite books, company contests, or fabulous trips to subtly show the great lifestyle available from being a part of your business.

Email: Weapon of Mass Communication

Most likely, your primary communications medium to the field is still email. Email is a wonderful marketing tool but will eventually fail to deliver for you if you send messy, ill-timed or untargeted messages.

With all the upline and downline messages, event notices, congrats, alerts, tidbits, and promotions your distributors receive, it's a wonder there's time for anyone to sell anything. Most email is almost instantly scanned and trashed. Only a few select messages are ultimately judged worthy of reading at all.

It's not just the volume of email that's a problem.. Most companies send email to the field in one-off, poorly-executed blasts that don't take the recipient's preferences or personal situation into account. Unsegmented email leads to poor response rates, lower event attendance, blocked emails, or worse: *frustration with you and what you have to say.*

© Copyright William Haefeli

"Oh no, we're being spammed!"

Your company's emails should generate excitement, increase leads and produce revenue. In order to get opened they need to shine through the clutter.

The best marketers plan and organize their email marketing campaigns. They engage their field with good content, and they know oodles about them and therefore have the ability to customize and make things personal.

Most of all, they are respectful of the recipient's inbox, which leads to higher open and response rates.

Don't give people another reason to turn away from you with something as simple as email. Step up your email marketing game and become a better emailer.

The Key to Successful Emailing? Try a Little Empathy

Successful email marketing is grounded by empathy. Ask yourself —do you like to be pitched every time you open an email? Do you enjoy receiving emails that seem written for someone else? Probably not, and neither does your field.

When eMail means eFAIL

If you're sending out random, all-encompassing "blast" emails, it means that you're not paying attention to the people receiving them. You're treating everyone like everyone else. And that means you're wasting time and money, and your campaigns won't work as well. Yes, it's more convenient and quicker to just hit the "send to all" button, but think of the recipient first. If they're the least bit annoyed (and it doesn't take much) what makes you think they're going to respond to your email?

Respect the Inbox

- **Segment and Target:** When emailing, rifles are far better than shotguns. Get to know exactly who your email list subscriber is and customize your email to them using data as a cornerstone of your campaigns. All email service providers have tools for segmenting lists in detail.
- **Measure:** Measurement is also critical. Your provider can provide detailed reports on opens and click-throughs; they'll tell you who is inter-

ested and who isn't. They'll tell you about your audience and what they like to see. Pay attention to the data to see what campaigns are working and which are duds, and adjust as needed.

- **Give them what they want:** Provide something of value, make your headlines work, and don't assume that just because you wrote it, it will be read. In fact, assume the opposite. And be sure that the person who creates your email is an astonishingly good writer who also understands network marketing. If you are using email just to push promotions and sales content, you'll fail. Give a reason to look forward to your messages. Humor is a great tool for capturing imagination as well. If your emails are dry and boring, they just won't get read.

- **Always be closing? No, always be *asking*.** It's important to stay on top of the preferences and attitudes of your subscribers. Gain permission first, then continue to ask what they like/dislike about your emails, and allow an easy way to unsubscribe. Always ask their opinions, and use the data to improve your campaigns. In any case, never email anyone who hasn't explicitly opted-in.

- **Find Your Center.** As a part of our client programs, we always set up a virtual "communications center" such as a blog or the backoffice, to serve as a primary source of information. This can minimize the need to send an email about every single little thing that happens. There are several advantages to this: the sites are owned by the client, they are a center where everyone knows they can get the latest information, they help the company rank for SEO, and they can be completely customized and branded. The sites feed and interconnect with all social and web properties as well.

- **Have Fun.** This industry is supposed to be fun, not tiresome. Believe it or not, getting an email can be exciting if it's done right. The best companies actually get their subscribers to look forward to their weekly, bi-weekly, or monthly missives. Sometimes they'll even send a note of thanks for a holiday special or surprise event. Think of it as an event, and then make sure it is an event for the audience. If you've run out of ideas, go get help.

- **Send Emails *From* Your Field.** Consider systems that email external prospects and customers on behalf of your field. Providers like IMN and others can create compliant, company sponsored newsletters that serve as relationship-builders between your distributor and prospects/customers. Email from a friend or acquaintance is going to be more effective than email from a company. This way, you can have the best of both worlds.

Whatever the Platform, Stand Out and Interact

As we've seen throughout this chapter about "social media tools," every tool and site is different. Facebook offers more room to move, *per se,* than Twitter, while Twitter provides more guardrails for your creativity and quicker access to other people. Pinterest allows people to share interests first. YouTube and LinkedIn both provide very different versions of social interaction, but can be just as valuable in the right hands. There are more, and more are coming.

All of these platforms should be examined up, down, and sideways, to find the unique ways they can show off your company's personality and connect with people.

The important thing is to be consistent. Get a routine down, and stick to it. If you have enough of a social following, and you're doing a good job of getting exposure for your business, folks will know what they're getting into when they happen upon your other social media sites.

Remember that it's not only about standing out.. It's also about being yourself; maintaining a culture, if not a brand, throughout your social media interactions. Use the tools to make yourself unique, and someone that other people want to follow.

The social web is noisy. What will make people notice you and want to join your cause? Some markets, like Gen Y, require additional ways of connecting.

Creative Emailing: Make the Boring Fun Again

What makes for great email? Fun, engagement, a bit of cheeky irreverence. The email below is from David Gonzales of Internet Marketing Party in Austin, Texas. His monthly emails are almost always aimed at getting me to attend his events or buy a premium subscription. But the strange thing is, I actually look forward to getting them. They are funny and interesting and get my attention. When I see the headline I want to know more.

David somehow finds a creative way, every month, to say the same thing over and over. I open every one, and as a result, I occasionally attend his events. Who knows, I may just subscribe too.

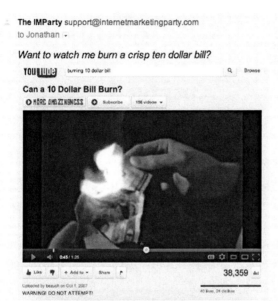

The IMParty support@internetmarketingparty.com
to Jonathan ⌄

Want to watch me burn a crisp ten dollar bill?

I would not do that, just because I'd rather give
it to my daughter or a good friend in need.

But if you have not gotten **your ticket to the party**
for tomorrow night (Thur, 2/16), and you plan on going,
then you'll essentially be setting flame to ten bucks.

Here's why...

1. Tickets for tomorrow's IMParty (with Carl White) **are $19 today**.
2. Tomorrow, they'll go up to $29.

The moral of this story?

Example of Email Creative: IMParty

Chapter 5

Connecting With GenY

MOST DIRECT SELLING COMPANIES HAVE NO idea what to do about the next generation of technology-dependent, short attention-span, want-it-all-now Generation Y. You know, the ones with the implanted headphones cranking out an average of 300 text messages a day? How can you get their attention, much less get them to sign on with your company?

Perhaps it would just be easier to not worry about the future and just enjoy the moment and bask in all the recent industry attention from the mainstream press. After all, the field will figure this stuff out and keep the engine humming...right?

Like it or not, these savvy young adults are the future of your company. Ignore them, and sooner or later your numbers will begin to slip as recruitment and retention get harder and harder.

Let's take a look specifically at how this generation challenges many of our assumptions so we can better prepare your business.

It's Bigger Than the Baby Boom

The challenge of how to adapt to GenY is more intriguing to me than any other trend in our industry. It also likely keeps many direct selling executives like you awake at night. This generation is already bigger than the baby boom and represents a tsunami of new attitudes, behaviors, demographics and preferences. And the wave is headed straight for your beach.

Unfortunately there are few easy answers. You can't just redouble your current efforts and reach GenY -- they aren't where you're reaching to begin with. You also won't get there simply by "hiring the young'ins" or setting up a Facebook page.

No, this challenge requires big thinking and the intestinal fortitude to make what could be sweeping changes in your marketing, systems, and core messaging. Your whole approach may be perfect for boomers, yet ring completely hollow for GenY.

> **"***You can't just redouble your current efforts and reach GenY — they aren't where you're reaching to begin with. You also won't get there simply by 'hiring the young'ins' or setting up a Facebook page.***"**

Because the generational differences are so profound, most established companies are likely to react too late and lose the chance to capitalize on what could be their greatest opportunity for growth ever in this industry. The changes may prove too uncomfortable for executives who just don't get how to capture the attention and imagination of young people.

Surely, you say, our industry has overcome huge challenges and has still wildly prospered. Hostile regulation, consumer distrust, high-profile lawsuits, we beat 'em all. One could even declare that the industry is even in a renaissance of sorts.

But GenY is a "megatrend", not just an issue of the day. Its cultural significance is vast and global and trumps anything we've seen. The reason? Technology of course, with its instant information, connectedness and mobility.

GenY presents a whole new set of circumstances that direct sellers must get in front of, or face slower growth or even irrelevance.

The future is here

First, some background. 93 million strong, GenY is now the largest generation in the United States today. Bigger than baby boomers at 76 million, GenY have an annual spending power of $1.5 trillion. Born between 1978 and 1993, most are beyond college-age. Though independent in their mindset, many are still supported by their parents due to higher debt loads they carry (an average of $25,000), combined with limited opportunity in the traditional work world during the great recession.

A few descriptors of GenY (we Gen-X'ers love labels): Casual. Entitled. Adventure-seeking. Collaborative. Tech-dependent. Impatient. Open. Creative. Fickle. Recognition-motivated. And, of course. Connected. Very connected.

They are the first to grow up entirely online, and from an early age they have extensively used personal computers, mobile phones, e-mail, video games and the Internet. Nearly all (95%) have a profile on Facebook and half own a smartphone. They instinctively lean towards technology for any solution they need, they're super-mobile and can be impatient with things they perceive could be better managed with technology, but aren't.

Addicted to Technology.

On a recent plane trip from a client's executive retreat, a young man about twenty-one years old took the seat next to me. As I watched him assemble his various gadgets and put everything together just so, we made chit chat about the topic of my presentation at the retreat, which happened to be about how to engage Gen Y. I asked him, "Just curious, if you had to choose, what would you rather lose, your technology or an appendage?" He sat back and carefully considered the question. "Hmmm. Appendage." "Do you care which?" I said. He

> *responded, "Well I'd prefer a foot, since I'd need my hands to use my technology. Although I have a friend who lost his forearm in Iraq and he's fine, because his phone is built into his prosthetic."*
>
> *That is more than tech-savvy, that's dependence. How long can your company go without addressing this astounding level of dependency on technology?*

GenY wield their beloved tech mightily. As much as you've read here about the benefits of communications technology to our industry, it is certainly a double-edged sword. GenY'ers instantly compare prices, reviews and reputation with the tap of a smartphone, making it easier for them to buy—and far more difficult to sell to them. They inquire with their networks and peers to learn about others' experience. They even check with their parents. And they love giving reviews of their experiences with brands, both positive and negative.

Are you lovable?

Since they have immediate access to independent information about your product or service, its competition, ingredients and pricing, you must focus on reasons for GenY to love you, your team, your culture and your "reason for being" as much as your financial opportunity or product.

Rob Snyder, Chairman of Stream Energy says

this love with GenY goes both ways, and that self-promotion is being replaced with engagement. "Our youth are craving the opportunities to bond with movements that present the opportunity to unite with causes larger than the collective sum." He went on to say "Companies who understand social media will best harness, on a pull basis, the naturally-existing desire of their constituents to unite, coalesce, and draw from the collective strength."

Indeed, cause and community are important identifiers of this generation.

With GenY, you must give them a reason to buy from you. You're selling your people and culture as much as you sell your product. Me-too brands are at risk—GenY knows they can choose from multiple options, so constant and rapid innovation is critical. Go ahead, give them something to love.

Your great challenge...and opportunity

For sure, appealing to this generation seems overwhelming. For direct sellers however, the opportunity is every bit as immense. Our model of marketing through networks and relationships happens to also be a defining characteristic of GenY. It is a whole population of people skilled at leveraging networks.

Think about it. GenY'ers have not known an unconnected world for most of their lives. Everyone they know is uber-networked, and reachable, with a keystroke. This very fact alone should whet the ap-

petite of anyone who appreciates the power of social networks. Namely, you.

Twenty-Five Actions You Can Take Now to Connect with GenY

So what can you do?

- **Present your opportunity in a way that appeals to GenY.** Address their dreams and anxieties. Our industry is uniquely positioned to appeal to GenY. Seeking independence? *Check.* Spending money? *Yep!* Adventures and fun? *In spades.* Social networking? *That's what we're all about!*

- **Review your recognition programs.** Does your reward match GenY aspirations? Does achievement (ranking up, bonuses, etc.) happen early enough to keep them engaged? Perhaps your rank names don't appeal as much to GenY. Are they motivated to earn a "Diamond", or is "Director" more appealing? It depends on your culture, but whatever the reward, let them know that you notice and appreciate their individuality and accomplishments.

Sample of online innovation: Mary Kay's groundbreaking virtual makeover tool.

- **Recognize, all the time.** You know why this is necessary. It's how GenY grew up. So give them the virtual blue ribbon for everything: Signed up? *Hooray!* Downloaded your first video? *Great work!* Made your presentation? *We've got to tell everyone!* This doesn't have to cost much, recognition can come in the form of a "badge" in the system or a phone call from the CEO, and definitely on social media. It just needs to be sincere. And constant.

93

- **Stand for important things.** What does the company stand for? Does it align? A good place to start with GenY is refreshing your approach toward the environment and other causes. Are your packaging, product or marketing materials wasteful? Does the company dedicate itself to helping people outside the organization? If the only thing your marketing demonstrates is a love of money, you'll miss this generation, not because they don't love money but because the association with a money message is unappealing.
- **Culture is vital.** Without a strong, empowering and connected culture you won't be able to retain GenY and fend off competitors. The culture comes from the top down, so you as CEO need to lead it. Just because you might be older doesn't mean you can't connect. It takes work and new messaging. Indeed if connecting is difficult, you may need to present a "face" to the field that can. Most of all, loosen up. Don't be the guy wearing a suit and tie at the pool party, unless of course it makes good video.
- **Take another look at your compensation plan.** Comp plans are a core factor in acquisition and retention and central to any culture building. Make sure your comp plan appeals to GenY, instantly gratifies, is recognition and achievement-

oriented and builds community and collaboration, rather than cutthroat competition.

- **Democratize your brand.** Provide a platform for GenY to create marketing content for the company and acknowledge them for it. For GenY'ers to feel a part of your company they should be encouraged to use their well-honed creative and collaborative strengths for the overall good of the company. Conversely, heavy-handed policing of your brand and marketing should be minimized. Unless it hurts the brand or is otherwise risky, consider allowing it or even praising it publicly. Give them a safe arena to create content and marketing materials on your own properties, and cheer for them!

- **Ramp up your social media efforts.** Without question, you must have a robust social media presence with GenY. GenY will look to their peers to offer opinion and approval of their decisions. Your social platform should provide opportunities for GenY to work the way they work. Do it right—a homemade Facebook page with a few "college tries" of content does more harm than good.

- **Respect their individuality.** GenY was raised on self-esteem and told that each one of them is special and unique. They believe it. Make it a part of your culture to notice and appreciate your field's individuality and accomplishments.

- **Rethink your own interaction styles.** One of the thing that sometimes annoys older counterparts is when GenY'ers split time between talking with you and answering the hundreds of text messages they exchange every day. Don't worry about it, they aren't trying to be disrespectful and are likely just as involved in the conversation as you are. And, if you send them signals that you're put off by their behavior, you likely won't connect with them.

- **Appeal to what is important to GenY.** Show them how your opportunity allows for people to create their own destinies. Flexible time at work, owning a business, mentoring, supporting causes, personal development, and education are all things GenY seeks.

- **Go modular in your product strategy.** With an audience that bores more quickly, innovation and new products are crucial. Design your products and packaging for quick revisions and add-ons.

- **Be transparent.** Don't fake anything, ever. Be up front with your field and let them know how you can help them. Don't hoard information; instead, divulge and disclose everything within reason.

- **Authenticity is crucial.** Anything you claim will be checked. Anything you say will be recorded. You must be genuine and your true self, both as a company and a leader. All of your messages should capture and embed the authentic core of the company. Also discourage your field from embellishing your story, it could come back to haunt you.

- **Work extra hard on on-boarding.** GenY'ers are inclined to quickly drop things that aren't showing immediate benefit. Compensation should reward behavior early and often, and live mentoring should be available to counter enrollment remorse.

- **Minimize barriers to enrollment.** Trials, samples and anything free are always good. Sizable enrollment fees and lock-in contracts are not appealing at all. Autoship programs should be easily started—and canceled. People who feel trapped become resentful very quickly.

- **Reward creativity.** Accolades for doing things outside the box should flow all the time. Provide multiple ways for creativity to be honored and rewarded. Channel creative energy to positive output, such as Facebook contests, video submissions, and other content that is fun for distributors and provides a constant feed of fresh user-generated content to the company.

- **Push technology to the limit and stay on top of it.** Your replicated sites should make a GenY'er proud, not embarrassed. This is no small achievement. Your distributor back office should be smooth and intuitive. If it's clunky and archaic or worse, frustrating, the company will be viewed similarly, at least from an operations standpoint.

- **Protect your reputation on search engines.** GenY of course lives online and when introduced to your company will immediately seek back up information. Who is this company? Who do I know is involved? What do they think of it? Most will make a decision right then and there and won't waste time drilling down if you don't pass this initial test. Your search results should be clean as a whistle, and your social media presence should provide plenty of opportunity for peer endorsement.

- **Meet them on their screens.** Anyone attempting to focus on GenY must meet them on all four screens, in addition to in-person. Selling tools should be digitally available and work on computers, mobile phones, tablets and TV screens. Your selling system and corporate sites should be optimized for mobile viewing, and sign-up should be easy to achieve on a tablet or smartphone. (See Chapter 6)

- **Don't waste time.** You must appeal to GenY's unique needs immediately, right then and there. GenY detest long-winded explanations of benefits when a quick effective summary of "what's in it for me" will do.

- **Review your current media.** Your team may be very sentimental about the 30-minute fire-side video from the founder, but if no one is watching what good is it? The maximum length of your videos should be no more than three (count 'em, three!) minutes or less. And even shorter for GenY.

- **Review your marketing materials.** Your web copy should be succinct and punchy, to the point. Sales materials should be similar in style to collateral you see in the mainstream. Think Apple, Starbucks, Abercrombie. Messaging should match GenY needs. Our industry is the perfect answer for them, they just don't know it yet.

- **Shorten it up, everywhere.** Make your videos, web copy, audio, and events fast-paced and fun so they stay interesting. At your events, use shorter stage segments, mix up the message so it's not the same for the entire event.

- **Re-evaluate products and services with GenY in mind.** Sensitivity to environmental concerns and all-natural ingredients are a minimal starting point. Questionable ingredients and ridiculous packaging will be called out immediately. Think of all your competitors and their distributors just looking for that one flaw in your product to post online.

GenY or No GenY?

Finally, and perhaps most importantly, consider if you can or should even play in this market. Though GenY is the future of the industry, perhaps it's not in *your* near future. If your products or proposition can't fit their lifestyle, you may opt to intentionally narrow your appeal to Boomers or GenX'ers. However, I would posit that this is a "smaller" strategy and growth expectations may need to be adjusted in the intermediate and long term.

GenY is the future. The future is fast, connected and mobile. You must be where they are and meet them on their terms to capture their imagination and dreams.

In the next several years, the vast majority of social activity and online commerce in general will be done from mobile devices. If your company has not formed a plan to address the mobile revolution, read on.

Chapter 6

Social Selling & Radical Mobility

"In a few short years, Earth will likely be home to more smartphones and tablets than human beings."
~ TheWeek.Com

THIS BOOK IS NOT JUST ABOUT social media and direct selling, it's also about *connectivity*. And within the next several years, connectivity will mean one thing—smartphones. Very soon, nearly all of your interactions with your field will take place on a mobile device.

The fact is nearly half of your distributors — and everyone they meet — are on a smartphone. With app usage now actually exceeding web usage for the first time ever, the demand for mobile accessibility and instant information gratification is on the rise.

Apps Should Prompt Action

Joe is standing in line for a latte. His phone buzzes tell-

ing him that Mary, who's in his downline, is one sign-up away from a fabulous cruise. Do you think Joe might hit the "Call Mary" button if it's right there in front of him? Most likely, he will. Mobile allows him to occupy time doing something meaningful and productive that would otherwise be wasted waiting in line. If a significant number of distributors do the same, it doesn't take long to realize what just a few actions a day could mean for the bottom line of your company.

This is only one small example of how mobile can be used to directly affect a company's volume and growth. Increasingly, there are entire suites of mobile value that could be accessed by your distributors — tools to make their efforts easier and more profitable for everyone.

Why Mobile Can't Wait

In the very near future, mobile technologies will become indispensable for direct selling companies. How can we grow our companies in an increasingly connected world while maintaining the human feel of our one-of-a-kind business model?

The bottom-line for increasing production is finding seemingly small, yet meaningful, ways to increase the number of actions by distributors. Effectively designed apps can drastically improve distributors' "information-to-action" ratio can lead to increased retention, production, revenue, and profit.

Direct sellers know that more actions inevitably translate into more recruiting, retention, and sales.

What are the primary benefits to implementing mobile apps to the field?

1. Increased Production. If your active distributors were able to easily increase their daily activity through two additional actions — a call here, a quick encouraging text there — what would that do for your revenue and retention? A well-designed mobile app can help distributors take effective action quickly. An app can tell them what to do now, in the moment. Hot leads or chance meetings can be acted on more quickly when there are simple in-app presentations and immediate in-app sign-ups. Additionally, with CRM (Customer Relationship Management) built into apps, chances are that your field will also follow up much more effectively than they did before. When you do the math, it's really a no-brainer.

2. Increased Retention. The holy grail. A good app can prevent new representatives from slipping through the cracks by alerting and reminding su-

Example of distributor mobile app:
LifeMax

104

per busy upline leaders to reach out to them at just the right times. It can also encourage new recruits to stick around longer by giving them simple tools to keep them focused and "in the know". The new daily method of operation will become enjoyable and consistent because they can now carry their business with them. Most of all, an app can make the often intimidating "sales" process of identifying and contacting prospects an easy, systemized experience.

3. Improved Onboarding. The ability to ramp up new recruits can be streamlined with the smart application of video and training systems to the small screen. This can sharply reduce the learning curve as well. Convenience is the key here — videos, podcasts, and presentations can be sent directly to the user's screen wherever they are without having to sit at a desk, find a computer or worry about having an internet connection.

4. Direct and Indirect Revenue. Your app could become a major source of revenue itself. A few dollars per distributor could mean a very lucrative, non-commissionable revenue stream for the company. Companies who prefer not to add another tool for the field to buy may consider adding it to their premium website packages or simply buy it for the field and add it to the tool set.

5. Indirect Revenue. That said, what is most compelling about apps is the amount of indirect revenue that could result from a more energized, active and efficient field. The revenue from a significant increase in adoption of mobile apps could pay for the initiative many times over. Even if you'd prefer not to sell tools to your field, chances are you will see a nice payoff of your investment fairly quickly in production alone.

6. Overcome Gen Y Barriers. As we discussed earlier, if you covet a younger audience your business must be mobile. Younger prospects simply will not join if they cannot manage their business on the go. Many decide to sign up based on the tools available to them. They want to know that there is a framework for success, and a good mobile app is a powerful way to communicate your sophistication as a company and demonstrate the support you offer to the field. The communication tools and networking functionality of many apps are particularly well suited for a GenY audience; constant communication and interaction is what they are all about. GenY need instant gratification to stay interested, and become impatient when they see manual or slow processes that could be improved with technology.

7. Leverage the Google and Apple Brands. Companies can realize a significant lift in branding just by offering apps through Apple and Google. Mobile is a great way to leverage their billions of marketing dollars for the benefit of your offering. The average consumer inherently trusts the apps that come from these great brands and some of that goodwill can transfer to your brand by association. Networkers are

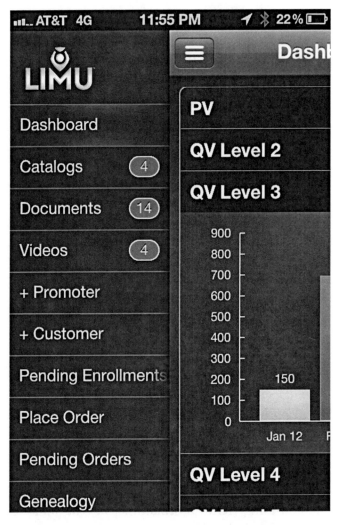

Sample of LIMU's mobile app interface: Personal Dashboard.

naturally attracted to companies that are ahead of the curve. Mobile app technologies can communicate innovation, dynamism, and competitive smarts.

8. Create System Dependency. Mobile apps can enhance and simplify field is training, making corporate-sponsored training much simpler to duplicate. New distributors will do the business the way they were brought in and trained. Mobile makes these tools available, in real time, to distributors wherever they happen to be, increasing their buy-in and reliance on company-vetted training and tools and eliminating some of the variations on training inherent in many companies.

9. Going Mobile Does the Right Thing by Your Field. By bringing the field what it wants and giving them the tools that they need, you are being responsive. And isn't that what we're all here for?

At some point in the near future not having a mobile application in your distributors' arsenals will be akin operating without a website. It's not a matter of if, it's a matter of when.

Mike Edwards, Director of Digital Marketing at Amway, shared the company's reasons for going mobile: "Mobile commerce is the future. Pretty much any consumer trend information you read today is pointing to the power of mobile." (Source: *Mobile Commerce Daily*, Dec. 2009) Powerful words about a powerful tool!

Be mindful of the mobile future as you design your Social Selling strategies. The mobile transformation of society cannot be ignored, and mobile should be part of your marketing and technology mix.

The New "Mobile University"

Mobile apps clearly have incredible uses for not only presenting in the field and signing people up, but motivating and spurring the behaviors that lead to results. Another powerful use? Training.

Unlike the old school days of creating your "university on wheels" via tapes and CDs, mobile apps bring a new vibrant aspect: interactivity. Training can be revolutionized and made more fun, with a higher uptake and level of comprehension.

Mobile apps also have the potential to drastically reduce training costs. Integrating and centralizing training resources and information is a relatively undeveloped, and potentially lucrative, area of app development in direct selling.

1. **Mobile apps offer a difficult-to-quantify yet powerful psychological advantage to distributors.** Most new entrants would prefer to appear as experts on their offering. However, many companies have expansive product lines or complicated compensation plans that make onboarding a real challenge. App technologies can provide access to entire product lines, giving distributors the ability to display them either overt-

ly or covertly to the customer, since they possess all of the information in the palm of their hand. This can help new reps appear informed and trained rather than fumbling through pamphlets and papers or being tied to a DVD player or computer.

2. **Companies still must think about the way new entrants learn.** Educational systems should increasingly integrate technology into the learning process. Using a large array of tools can target the differences in learning styles and dramatically reduce the time, cost, and headaches of the learning curve. Younger generations are especially accustomed to this kind of learning.

3. **A distributor can gain access to selling tips** or parts of their sales message right on their phone, without it being apparent to the prospect. Even if he or she doesn't need to access this information, simply knowing they could can provide a dose of confidence and reduce anxiety.

4. **App technologies can streamline training processes.** Interactive guides or step-by-step information manuals can be developed to show less experienced distributors how to demonstrate products or appeal to customers and prospects. Apps can enable the communication channels for questions and answers in real time. Each additional bit of available information makes action that much more likely to happen, wher-

ever distributors are. Simple daily reminders can share valuable guidance from the pros and help new recruits keep focused, reduce confusion, and reinvent the meaning of retention.

Mobile has great potential for training on the go. Downtime can be filled with training material, not just "on wheels" but everywhere. The extreme mobility and interactivity afforded by apps creates broad opportunities to keep your sales systems, training, and inspirational messages in front of your field, leading to increased buy-in, better on-boarding and higher success overall.

Being There in Spirit — And Pixels

Of course Radical Mobility means a field on the go when and where they want to be. It's about the freedom to be where you want to be and still get stuff done. I would argue that kind of freedom and direct selling's promise of freedom go hand in hand.

Again, a perfect match for Social Selling.

Another aspect of the expansive reach of technology is the ability to bring our experience to people wherever they are, whether on some distant island or right at their kitchen table. How many people across the world want in attending your events or visiting your office who for whatever reason can't be there in person? Should you discriminate against travelers vs. non travelers? Or against people who can't afford to drop a grand or two on expenses? Of course not. We love 'em all! We all know how disappointed a lot of folks in the field can be when they can't get to an important event. Happens every time we hold an event.

How can we bring the excitement of an event or the effectiveness of in-person training to the people who can't or prefer not to be there in person?

Well hold on to your hats, because we are very near the virtualization of a lot of what we do.

Broadcast Yourself—Live

One of my clients recently asked me what it would take to broadcast an event so their entire field could watch it. They had a very special "remembrance" event in mind, a commemoration for the company founder who had passed away the year before. Because of technical and bandwidth hurdles it was not quite the right time (they chose to record the event and post it instead.) However it was not lost on us how important this idea is, or how close this is to being commonplace for direct sellers.

Platforms such as UStream and LiveStream offer live streams to anyone. Gamers showing live competitions, pirate news stations, people with similar interests just talking with each other. Now Google has now introduced "hangouts", super easy-to-use live video meeting rooms for the masses.

Take it up a notch, and think about the many things your company might want to stream live to the field. Conference calls could get a boost with live video broadcasts. Annual convention keynotes, training workshops, community events and anything that is done in the name of excitement and buzz can be broadcast live.

Not Your Father's Webinar

Now, take it up another notch. Five years ago I came close to partnering with a provider of virtual training systems and was amazed at the possibilities of virtual worlds when it came to events and training. Now, it's everywhere. Virtual world technology is already being used extensively by the Army (Source: *US DoD*) and by corporate trainers to teach, inform and gather people from far flung areas across the world.

Virtual worlds (like the online game Second Life) are three-dimensional, fully interactive experiences. Imagine you've just walked into your company's rally...more accurately, your avatar, or virtual person, walked into a virtual rally. The room is full of other avatars, many representing your real-life "team". You take a seat and chat (text chat, that is) with nearby neighbors while waiting for the company president's avatar to get on the stage. You may see your good friend across the room and give her a virtual high-five!

Oh the virtual excitement!

When the company president arrives, his real voice is broadcast live to your computer speakers

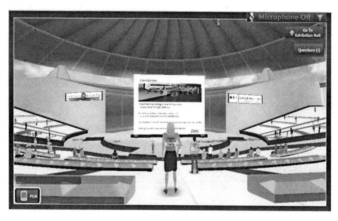

and the crowd goes virtually crazy (typing like mad into their chat boxes that sit above their heads). Soon enough you are immersed in this world—it all seems so *familiar*—and you briefly forget that you're in your real home with your real cat in your real lap.

I can already hear industry purists grumbling about how this type of technology won't cut it in the excitement and momentum-building category. True, it may pale in comparison to pressing the flesh and whopping it up in person. But what I'm talking about here is not replacement of real human relationships. Just as social media enhances and expands relationships without replacing them, virtual worlds can do the same thing.

One client we are working with is considering a standing monthly virtual "event" as a unique way to introduce the company to others. It's the equivalent of their opportunity calls and since the program is pretty much the same, it won't take much work to put them together regularly after the platform is built.

Let's do the math. Company X has 100,000 reps. They expect maybe 5,000 to attend convention. Now you might assume another three or four thousand would love to go but can't. How many of those would log on, for just part of the time, if the meeting were broadcast? How many more who wouldn't normally go would log on for at least part of the event? And how many who would log on just to be there when the big announcement breaks, or to attend a workshop they were interested in? A few thousand more perhaps? That's a few thousand real people, taking time to learn and participate about you and your company. Your reach expands.

What about the guests your field might invite? Think a few people might show up? Maybe they'll hear your message and want more, or maybe it's all they needed to sign up!

Remember, the young and tech-savvy will love you for this kind of stuff. Progressive, cool, forward-thinking and using technology in a smart way.

The rise of virtual worlds for business use opens up interesting opportunities for our companies. I am confident several reading this book with talk with their team the next day and start to explore virtual worlds for events, training and marketing. Why not?

Chapter 7

Tips for Winning in Social Media Internationally

Cheers! or ¡Salud! Sláinte! Prost! Kampai!
乾杯！干杯！

EARLIER THIS YEAR I SAT IN on a client's annual convention and it was a blast. Lots of energy and fun for this company that does a large amount of its business in places like China, Korea and Mexico. Which got me thinking, how can we capture all this excitement in far-flung countries via the social web, as we do in the US?

Believe it or not, millions of people outside the US are using social media, and a large number of them aren't using it the same way we are.

Facebook, with its billion+ users is the big kahuna of social media and the most popular site worldwide.

However it is not at all the only game in town, er, world. Ever hear of NetLog? The most popular social site in Europe. Yanja.com? Number one in the

116

Middle East. Habbo is huge…in Finland.
Clearly, one network does not fit all.

> **❝** *The number one driver for social media activity in China is not personal updates or photo sharing, it's social gaming. Indeed, Farmville began in China!* **❞**

Example of an international social site: RenRen in China.

Preferences vary internationally, as social networking can be an intimate thing. Some social media platforms are more appealing in some cultures than others, some do not "feel right", and some are more intuitive in a particular context. For instance, the number one driver for social media activity in China is not personal updates or photo sharing, it's social gaming. Indeed, Farmville began in China!

This is why connecting with international audiences on social media takes time and resources to get it right. You just don't know that what you do at home will work abroad.

So what are global companies doing to reach and engage countries abroad other than hoping many of them login to their US-based Facebook page? It turns out not much. This creates opportunities for savvy global-minded companies to get in front of a phenomenon that is becoming as powerful a medium abroad as it is in the US. If your company is focused on new business in new countries, the opportunities for Social Selling to help increase momentum are significant.

As you can imagine there are issues of consistency, regulations, cultural sensitivity and most of all, cost. But the opportunity exists to engage with people where they spend a significant amount of their time networking with others.

Depending on the countries where you have distributors, you may need to adapt service in multiple languages, up to fourteen for many truly global companies. Naturally this presents hurdles in the "immediacy" elements of social media. How does the CEO tweet in 14 languages? How does one parse what needs to be said in one country, refine for culture and language differences, post it all, and still keep wind in the sails?

There are ways to duplicate successful efforts at home to effective social marketing abroad:

- **Hire locally.** Assuming a support infrastructure in the countries of focus, we recommend you hire a social media manager in the country who reports to the country manager or the lead corporate rep there. This person will be familiar with languages, customs, can "keep it fresh" and serve as a liaison for the company. Careful though, this could become a high-profile position in the field; social should be ultimately managed by the home office where possible.

- **Act locally, even when virtual.** An alternative would be to hire a native-speaker for each country to work from the corporate office. Aside from time differences (important in social media), location should not matter so much. However, from HQ it is easy to get too narrowly focused on the home convention, events, field leaders, etc. In this case, the company should take care the "presence" is felt in the *host* country, not the home country. The manager should report to the country leader in any case. Though likely more expensive to hire at home, there are great advantages in being close to the executive team and being up to date on products, marketing and corporate news.

In either scenario, the social media manager of a country should absolutely be native-speaker and native born, hopefully someone who lives at least part of their regular lives in that country.

The freshness and transparency of social media means no faking it; the person is an extension of the company and any half-heartedness will show through.

Chapter 8

The Importance of Storytelling

"After nourishment, shelter and companionship, stories are the thing we need most in the world." ~ Philip Pullman, The Golden Compass

IN 1906 A MAN STARTS A *brush company in his basement, leading to a legendary home products firm.*

A visit to China in the 1920's prompts the invention of the multi-vitamin, leading to a $10 billion global sales powerhouse.

An entrepreneurial woman leaves the corporate rat race after a man she had trained gets promoted over her and builds a multibillion-dollar cosmetics company.

What do Fuller Brush, Amway, and Mary Kay have in common?

A great story.

Story is a big part of your corporate identity; your field uses it as a cornerstone in what they do. They

121

depend on simple, cogent stories to repeat and share with others so that they too may become enthralled with the company and/or its leaders.

Through stories, companies tell:

- **Who they are**
- **Where they come from**
- **Where they're going**

- **What they do**
- **How they do it**
- **Why they do it**

Why do people respond so strongly to stories? It's simple. Stories are universal. We talk in stories. Everyone loves a great story, and especially a great storyteller. Stories are what move people. A great story can mean the difference between a beloved company and an also-ran.

Social media goes beyond the pictures, words, or people. These are all pieces of the puzzle, of course. When the whole thing comes together and functions as one tool, you have the true driver of social media: content.

Craft your story early, and keep it consistent. Highlight the important parts, and keep it entertaining. Make sure anyone who's part of your Social Selling program lives and breathes the story you want to present, including your corporate history and the founders' or executives' personal histories.

Your Bite-Sized Social Media Story

Your story is also the foundation for your social media interactions. In fact your story is even more important in Social Selling.

A few years ago I attended a Direct Selling Association workshop led by Mark Stastny, Chief Marketing Officer at Scentsy, who was presenting on the company's marketing and social media efforts. I recall being impressed with how important the story of Scentsy was to their marketing strategy, how it permeates everything they do.

At some point I asked Mark how he fit Scentsy's epic story into one minute videos on tiny screens and in 140 characters. His answer was brilliant – "the story is the same, it is just proliferated and shared in bite-sized pieces, depending on the medium." So they tweet something about the barn they started the company in, and share it across platforms, re-working it for each platform, so that it is accessible and makes sense.

The great news is you need not compromise on your stories, or dumb them down or gut them. Stories should remain full and detailed; we can just divide them up a bit and serve as hors d'oeuvres rather than steak. They can both sizzle in their own way.

In Social Media, Content is King

To win in Social Selling companies must put forward a sincere and creative effort to amuse, entertain, and engage others with consistent content.

The thing about content is that it is unique to your company and should stem from your vision, mission and story. This is where your personality comes into play again. You have to make it personal and unique, and you have to give it meaning. What are people gaining from you that they can't find elsewhere?

The media may change, but your authentic story shouldn't. It's who you are, it's what people attach themselves to.

Despite popular misconceptions, legends aren't built of hyperbole and exaggeration. Consistent, authentic, and creative self-expression will build a public sense of trust. There's no need to overly-embellish a story and pretend it's the truth. Everyone has a great story; sometimes it just needs help to come to life. In this new anti-hype world, your story—personal, professional, corporate, or otherwise—must be authentic to resonate.

Hype Versus Authenticity: No More Impossible Promises

Looky here! This is the most incredible subchapter you will ever read! It's going to revolutionize the industry!! It's so stupendous we are running out of exclamation points!!!

If people seem skeptical about your offering or reject your product or promise out of hand, or choose not to interact with you, it may have something to do with what I call "impossible promises." In fact, your messaging may be turning people off.

"But Jonathan!" you say. "We like using the word

'revolutionary!' It gets people's attention and helps them learn how exciting and revolutionary we are!"

Good ideas are important, but impossible promises are counterproductive and do exactly the opposite of what is intended. Overly excited promoters turn people off, no matter how revolutionary the idea. Hype, in my opinion, can actually *slow* momentum.

People are naturally averse to hype in their personal lives, in politics, and *especially* from network marketers. Perhaps it's the industry's larger-than-life personalities, or maybe our unfounded fear that if we don't scream about something it won't be heard. Direct selling messages can become loud and overbearing at times.

This gets worse when we add social media to the mix. The net result is that the direct selling industry struggles to overcome its image as an over-promiser and under-deliverer. The habit of hype sends brand trust to the bottom of the consumer barrel, alongside infomercials and political campaigns.

Toward Authenticity

When you look at the most successful direct selling companies, what do you see? The best companies say what they mean and do what they say. Their message is consistent, authentic, and value-driven, and gives cause for belief rather than skepticism. These companies minimize the use of adverbs. They don't over-sell their products, and they don't make outra-

"On the Internet, nobody knows you're a dog."

geous statements. They make realistic promises – as real people would do – and let their products and services speak for themselves.

This doesn't mean that we need to change who we are or mirror big, boring, corporate America. Excitement and possibility is what direct selling is all about, so we need to find a good balance. It's time to stop promising to revolutionize everything, and start being "optimistically honest." We need to establish credibility, lay down paths to the greater vision, and appeal to logic and reason as often as we do emotion and imagination.

Even new entrants to direct selling understand this. Charlie Poznek, CEO at Rocky & Bella, says "A core strategy of ours is to leverage all social media technologies to create relationships based on trust and transparency."

You should discourage any boasting, bragging, and egoism both in and out of your company. It's not good for business. And it especially doesn't look good on social media. Your corporate marketing should follow a set of guidelines to keep things friendly and believable. The more friendly and believable you are—as opposed to loud and hype-y—the more people will be open to hearing you, and the more your field will mirror that behavior.

> **"** *It's time to stop promising to revolutionize everything, and start being 'optimistically honest.' We need to establish credibility, lay down paths to the greater vision, and appeal to logic and reason.* **"**

In the end, the more human your company seems, the more likely people are to connect with you and start interacting. What's more, the field will pick up on the corporate tone and messaging and make it their own, for the most part.

Be real, be flawed, be human. Allow people to see that you're just like them. No one is perfect – that's what makes us interesting and ultimately believable. Self-deprecation can go a long way; other people are self-conscious about not being perfect and they appreciate someone who can share their frustrations with humor and grace. These days, perfection is easy to find in technology, and as a result people are searching constantly for what's real, and that's where we're in luck; because what's real is what's us.

That's what's going to draw them to you.

Through the Looking Glass: Authentic Leadership is Key

One major cultural influence of the industry has been the rising significance of our public personas to our businesses. One industry leader truly understands this and its impact on our industry.

Founded in 2011, LIFE is an ambitious venture of lifelong networker and leadership author and trainer Orrin Woodward. Orrin, winner of the 2011 IAB Top Leader Award and LIFE Founder, has created a substantial and unique following among people intensely interested in improving not only their finances but their approach to life as a whole, hence the name.

"The fact is, social media and Internet search are two of the biggest game changers we've ever seen in our business," he says. "The difference between a positive or negative social profile and Google search can now mean the difference between a thriving business or failing one."

As a network marketing field leader, Orrin has had his share of public stresses famously hashed out several years ago in a lawsuit with his previous company. He has hard won experience in fighting all-too-pubic battles.

"In the end, the only way to treat those kinds of experiences is from your heart," he says. "In today's transparent age, everything a leader in our industry does will hit the web, so to be successful we must live our lives as if we can write all of it in the sky for others to read and discuss. These days, the act of hiding can be far more harmful online than the thing hidden."

"It's incumbent on leaders to put it all out there and be honest at all times. They can expect to be called out on anything and everything they do." Orrin explains that authentic leadership is a non-negotiable with social media, further eliminating the separation between a leader's public and personal lives.

"If you play the game with honor, social media will magnify your message, extending your influence beyond

what you previously thought possible. Archimedes said, 'Give me a place to stand and with a lever long enough and I will move the whole world.' Social media is the tool for leaders to leverage in reaching the whole world. Our society is reverting to its origins of trust, friendship and earnestness, because of this tool."

"Trust has gone high tech." he says, "And that's a good thing."

Chapter 9

Risk and Lawyers and Meanies, Oh My!

WITH ALL THESE GREAT NEW CHANNELS and opportunities for widespread communication, there comes a certain measure of risk. Networkers are increasingly using the Internet and Social Media to help them promote their businesses, and with ever-increasing enforcement from regulatory bodies like the FTC and FDA, the online environment presents new challenges.

In recent years there have been several very clear examples of companies being severely damaged as a result of income or product claims being made online by the field.

Other risks are more reputational. Due to the very nature of the Internet, anyone with a laptop can suddenly become a real problem for your company. Our industry in particular is besieged with what I call "Online Meanies," people whose reckless, irresponsible or just plain mean online comments can have a deleterious effect on a company.

The Rise of Online Meanies

What could be more discouraging than working all day to build trust and excitement about your company, then seeing the company and its leaders bashed and persecuted online? Or introducing all your friends and family to what you think is a great opportunity for them, but they keep bringing up that one thing they found on the Internet?

Picture this: Mary introduces her good friend Sally to your opportunity. Sally becomes excited and soon can't wait to get started. She runs home and does a quick check for the company name on Google to learn more.

What does she see? It's very possible words like "sucks" "scam" "struggling?" "get sales leads!" pop up on her screen.

Sally's excitement starts to wane, and she slowly loses trust in the opportunity...and in Mary. When Mary calls back to get Sally enrolled, Sally awkwardly explains that, well, she really doesn't have the time right now...

The direct selling industry is fertile ground for attacks and misleading information. Why? We're easy targets. We have some baggage. Litigation. Regulatory actions. Bad press. We've had it all.

"I just feel fortunate to live in a world with so much disinformation at my fingertips."

We also have more to lose. Our companies are more vulnerable to negative online search results than almost any other type of industry.

One angry ex-distributor or mlm-hater can wreak havoc on direct sellers and cost millions of dollars in recruitment and retention. Entire companies have nosedived as a result of unrestrained, malevolent complaint forums and non-stop wrist spasms from bloggers with too much time on their hands.

In recent years, the Direct Selling Association and Direct Selling Education Foundation have done a superb job of enhancing and improving the image of direct sellers and the industry at large. They've bought ads, produced outstanding educational programs and charmed the press. As a result, the newest generation of distributors and customers has fewer negative preconceived notions of the industry.

I would offer that the next big step we can take in the direction of improving the industry's image is to address the negative and often iniquitous comments, posts and blogs about our companies, model, and industry. I believe the negativity online is one of the single biggest image problems we face—its pervasiveness directly affects the growth of our companies. One bad link can steer away hundreds or even thousands from an opportunity, instantly.

Protecting Consumers, or Profiting From Negativity?

One of the more pernicious challenges is the advent of "complaint sites" and discussion forums dedicated to serving as supposed advocates for the downtrodden consumer.

66 *The next big step we can take in the direction of improving the industry's image is to address the negative and often iniquitous comments, posts and blogs about our companies, our model and our industry.* 99

Search the name of many leading direct selling companies and chances are one of these complaint sites is right there in the top ten or twenty results. This affects the best, most reputable companies in the industry. Mary Kay Corporation, for instance, is a victim of a custom complaint site which is ranked on the front page of their Google results. It's disturbing that such great companies doing such wonderful things for people could be so vulnerable to misrepresentations from in many cases, nutcases and cranks.

The rise of custom attack blogs and online complaint boards like RipOffReport.com and Scam.com, combined with negative search engine results is one of the most challenging areas for direct sellers today.

There is no doubt that negative rankings impact the bottom line, and the sooner they are addressed the better. Without early intervention and proper management of search results, companies risk the

Example of complaint board: Scam.com.

erosion of revenue, brand and the confidence of the public at large.

So what drives people to create and produce these sites? For the most part, they're aimed at driving traffic in order to generate income from Internet advertising. Other times they've got an ax to grind, or they're just crazy.

So what's an honest direct selling company to do to protect itself from such nastiness? At our firm we counsel our reputation management clients that there are things they can do to guard against and even repair the actions of damaging forums and blogs:

1. **Prevention is far better than repair.** All companies should strive to prevent people from seeing negative links to begin with, by creating strong search engine results pages under their brand name. This takes planning and investment. To not protect your brand name search results is tantamount to holding open mic night at your convention for any stranger who feels like talking about you.

2. **Actual repair of problem search results** takes a lot of time and even more money, often ten times the cost of prevention. It takes expertise, sophisticated (read: expensive) tools, and plenty of tedious work and elbow grease. It cannot be done effectively in house. I've had several clients who've come to us after long and wasteful efforts

of setting up websites, blogging, backlinking and other activities. Once you're under attack, you need to call in Special Ops.

3. **Google is an unpredictable beast.** You can spend months working on the problem, they make one small tweak to their algorithm and you're back at square one. This can only be answered by doing things the right way, naturally and over time. Tricks may work for a while, but Google catches up with them eventually and penalizes them. (Recently, Google updated its algorithm and up-ended the online reputation world. Our work was not affected—thankfully—but the black-hats and blog networks, which most of our competitors use, got killed.) A long-term strategy of real traffic, real authorship and real interaction is almost always rewarded.

4. **Search Engine Optimization (SEO) is NOT Reputation management.** Many SEO firms will tell you they can do rep management. Most can perform only one part of reputation management—the SEO part. There are many more, even non-technical aspects to online reputation. It's a profession more than technical trade.

Things You Can (and Should) Do to Protect Your Good Name

1. **Establish and maintain a robust social presence.** Google heavily favors social media, es-

pecially YouTube and Google Plus (go figure). Those links absolutely should show up on page one for your name. If they aren't showing up, you need to increase your activity and interactivity. (Reference the rest of this book!)

2. **Create good content, consistently.** Publish to your blog at least twice a week and constantly refresh any and all website properties.

3. **Link all your properties together.** The website to social, social to blog, blog to external websites, etc. They should all be working in concert.

4. **Produce lots of good video, and promote it to your field.** The more people who click on, watch and comment on your videos the better the chances it will rise to the top 10 on your search results.

5. **For problematic cases, you'll need a firm with deep reputation management experience in direct selling.** Check references specifically for reputation repair skills.

6. **Careful when communicating about any issues.** Whether you post to the offending blog or, as I've seen many companies do, attempt to control the message by writing a "private" memo (no such thing) to your field, anything you say as a company can be used against you. When you write anything, ask yourself what the devil himself would do with it. Would he say, "You know you're right, I'll take the blog down." Or would

he flagrantly mock it, violate your privacy, post misleading interpretations and make a sarcastic videos about it?

7. **Consider legal action— as a last resort.** By the time companies seek our help they are usually out for blood. Though it is one weapon in the arsenal, legal action is often ineffective and can be risky. Because courts have deemed a lot of what bloggers do "free speech", options are few and winning a lawsuit is unlikely unless someone has broken the law. Worse, litigation strategies can cast the true victim as an aggressor online, adding fuel to the fire. Be careful of over-reliance on attorneys, most do not have practical experience in this area and are often either too quick to sue or advise you to ignore it, hoping it will go away. It won't.

8. **Be patient.** There is no immediate cure for bad search results, primarily because the search engines penalize concentrated efforts to game the system. They reward natural online behavior and punish obvious attempts to manipulate.

The Internet has made it easy for Meanies and anyone else who feels dissatisfied to do serious damage to companies and reputations. Who are these people, and what can we do to head off their influence?

How to Handle Online Meanies and Complainers

I believe that there are five types of complainers, each of whom demand a distinct and appropriate response. Below I describe them and the responses which we at our firm find most useful.

1. Legitimate Complainers: These folks may have a legitimate gripe and even though they may be telling the truth, the posts can still be very mean-spirited. Maybe a shipment was late, or they had a bad experience with the company. Here are a few ways you can redirect their complaints into more positive exposure for your company:

- Engage the poster in an authentically helpful way.
- Explain the problem.
- Fix the problem quickly.
- Report a successful fix to the poster and forum.
- Ask if the original poster has anymore comments, issues, or concerns.

2. Unrealistic Expectation-ers: These folks are valued customers or distributors, however, as many of us know, they can sometimes ask for a bit too much. From not getting an immediate support response to a question to just being wrong about something. In this case it is best to be forthright and reasonable in your responses.

- Engage and explain, as above.

- The goal is to inform others, not necessarily fix the problem.
- Be careful of over-apologizing, as capitulation could set a precedent and sustain the unreasonable expectations.

3. Lunatics: These are the ones who are crazy, in it for the money, or are just plain unhappy with life. For whatever reason they want to take it out on you and your company. They live in the online equivalent of troll caves (complaints boards) and demand responses to riddles you can never answer.

- Engaging these people is like wresting with a pig; you both get dirty—and the pig likes it.
- Any response should be aimed at other readers, not the lunatic.
- You still may want to respond to inform others, however be careful to not fuel the fire.
- Be absolutely honest and truthful—or suffer the consequences when someone calls you out on it.
- Be fair and have good intentions, but don't expect that to help too much.
- If you respond, keep emotions out of it, and have neutral parties read your response before you post.
- Consider legal approaches – but very carefully.
- Attack with online reputation techniques.

4. Former Employees or Field Reps: We all know these folks. Disgruntled ex-employees and/or field reps can be "bloggers scorned" once they discover the power of the Internet!

- Usually easy to spot, both for the company and for readers.
- May be worth responding to in order to inform others.
- Warning: may morph into a Lunatic.

5. Press/Media: The search engines love announcements from real news agencies and government agencies – which is not good news if you find your company in regulatory hot water. If the negative link has a .gov extension on it (FTC.gov, FDA.gov, SEC.gov, you get the picture) or is proudly hosted on the Wall Street Journal's or New York Times site, it could be years before it leaves your search results on its own, if ever. In this case you'll want to:

- Use standard PR interface techniques.
- Ask for correction, if and when appropriate.
- Ask the site to include or rebut with your point of view.
- Attack with online reputation techniques. These links are difficult and costly to move, but it can be done.

Regardless of how squeaky clean you, your company, leaders and distributors are, all companies will face this issue at some point. The best approach is al ways to own up, be honest, respond in a smart way, and try and keep things on perspective.

Social Media and Compliance: How to be Great at Both

Of course with networkers increasingly using the Internet and Social Media to help them promote their businesses, risk becomes a concern. Too often, uncontrolled or unmonitored marketing by the sales field can have disastrous effects on your brand and your company.

Indeed, one of the greatest ongoing threats to any direct selling company's ongoing operations is an action by a governmental organization based on overblown income or product claims made by distributors. Regulatory actions can be a major distraction and can thrust the company into chaos.

In our industry, even a simple warning letter can be disastrous as it can kill momentum and field morale … and in our business, morale is everything.

While the openness of the Internet makes compliance incredibly difficult, it cannot be ignored. You must plan and enforce policy in order to protect your company.

Is a Facebook Page the same as a website?

Last year, just before I was due to speak at a client's convention, the company's compliance director asked if she could "prep" me prior to stepping onstage. After the

143

standard "what the heck are you going to say up there" questions, she explained to me that it wouldn't at all be necessary to discuss Facebook business pages because such pages were forbidden and ran afoul of policy.

When I asked what it was about business pages they didn't like, she explained to me that they were "the same as personal websites, and we don't allow them either." Needless to say, as popular as Facebook (and websites, for that matter) are for distributors in the field, this may have gutted my talk just a smidge.

But I took this as a teaching moment. Once I explained that a business or "fan" page was really just another way to express oneself and simply worked differently, she eventually came around and allowed me to describe the concept from stage.

I understand the concern. The company did not want to run the risk of out-of-compliance web sites doing damage to everyone who's associated with the company. Her company's approach was a "don't go there at all" tactic.

But how can we not go there? It's where everyone is! With a clear set of guidelines and enforcement of policy, social media can be far less risky than one might think.

So how can direct selling companies avoid the regulator's wrath? It's best to start at home.

1. **Monitor the Internet—in real time.** Sounds rather daunting to monitor the entire world,

doesn't it? There are tools and services that can greatly expand your company's ability to monitor for risky claims and keywords. While you should be doing this for marketing purposes anyway, the establishment of an online monitoring mechanism is a compliance necessity, especially if your field is fond of marketing online. A simple Google Alerts account can get you a lot of coverage, and there are also dedicated compliance monitoring services, such as our firm's FieldWatch™ and other programs you may want to consider.

2. **Prevent re-creation of the wheel.** Distributors are natural marketers and tend to create their own websites and materials, especially if those provided by the company are insufficient in their eyes. One way to prevent this is to create such compelling and appealing materials that they never feel the need to create their own non-compliant versions, thus exposing the company. There are great tools and technologies available that allow customization of replicated sites and social content, providing effective, compliant and approved content for your field. Look into tools you can provide that will manage the need for the field to create sales materials on their own.

3. **Rein in rogue distributors.** Naturally, some companies may resist admonishing individual

distributors for fear of upsetting the sales apple-cart. However it is critical to monitor, enforce, and document field claim issues. The well-known case at Mannatech was a classic example of "distributors gone wild," and it hurt the company tremendously. (They have since made an amazing recovery.) Make sure this doesn't happen to your company. Enforce your policies.

4. **Act swiftly and decisively when addressing claims issues.** No matter the rank or revenue, a distributor making false income claims or health claims online must be addressed immediately, up to and including pulling their distributorship. Some companies go further and actually make examples of leaders who blatantly violate claims restrictions, with the message being that anyone, even top leaders, can lose their business if they don't follow the rules that protect everyone.

5. **Deputize your field.** Your field can be your most valuable tool in enforcement. After all, their business is at risk from false claims just like everyone else's. Educate your field consistently about how it's in their best interest to police and report policy violations as they encounter them. Make them your allies.

6. **Restate and repeat.** Make "we all play by the rules and we all win" part of your company's culture. Make sure the field is clear on what it can

and cannot do and what the consequences are.

7. **Forge a strong compliance department.** If you agree that your compliance department is the only thing standing between you and the abyss, be sure that it's staffed appropriately and fully empowered to do its job. If your compliance director is squirreled away in a corner, with no real authority, it's only a matter of time before something hits the fan. One rule of thumb is that no one should be allowed to override a compliance decision, other than the CEO or General Council.

8. **Don't panic.** Unfortunately, occasional inquires and actions are a cost of doing business in our industry. There are financial, economic, and political reasons why agencies tend to target network marketing companies. Companies who are truthful and forthright in their marketing and sales will weather the storm, while the fly-by-nights or solely recruitment-driven companies get hit hard, not only with fines but with a fickle field seeking new pastures.

Chapter 10

Online Ads as Brand Defense

NOW FOR ANOTHER QUESTION IN REGARD to online media: Should your direct selling company generate its own online leads? Even (gasp!) run pay-per-click ads?

Yes, but not for reasons you might think.

Online ads may work for some industries, but a long-held tenet of direct sellers is that our companies don't advertise – that's what the field is for, right? "We don't spend money on ads, we pay commissions instead" is the mantra.

It is true that advertising doesn't align well with our model of personal selling. And as a result, most direct selling companies do not actively market their opportunities online. They are sensitive to the idea of "going around" the field and breaking the no-ads taboo. The idea of procuring leads on the Internet seems cheap somehow, and counterintuitive.

However, the Internet is far too integrated into our industry now. Online advertising should be considered, not necessarily to generate leads (though there are certain situations, like a company launch, where this works really well), but to protect the company image, support policy and compliance.

Marketers are Swarming Your Brand

The reality is that savvy online networkers have already discovered how to market online. And they're doing it *en masse*, on the back of your brand. Their intent may be good, but their activity is mostly uncontained and therefore not closely monitored by the companies they're promoting. As a result, many distributors' online efforts go against policy, recruiting cross-line or making non-compliant claims. That's not good for the company or the field. In fact, most of

"Fleming, bookmark that site."

the time distributors fail at online ads, which means they spend money and get nothing for it.

Another issue with online ads and search engine optimization is the prevalence of competitors and thousands of third-party bottom-feeders who ride the backs of the companies by using ads under their brand names. This diverts business, harms revenue and dilutes the image companies work so hard to build. I consider any third party advertising against a brand name to be outright competition, and it should be addressed.

Own Your Brand Online

Your company needs to own the acquisition of Internet leads under its name to protect its brand, not necessarily to market its business. Online ads for direct selling companies are a proven method for helping control the way your company appears in search. You may not wish to market yourself this way, but you can certainly benefit from the protection they afford.

I suggest to our clients that they start by jumping in and buying "branded" online ads and other strategies. Buying your own brand name in search engines is not overly expensive (ads are sold on an "auction" basis), and as a nice side benefit it can drive up ad prices for unfriendlies who advertise against your name.

Don't let the bottom-feeders own your search results.

Chapter 11

Adapt or Die!

"Playing it safe. Following the rules. They seem like the best ways to avoid failure. Alas, a dangerous pattern. The current marketing 'rules' will ultimately lead to failure. Fitting in is failing. In a busy marketplace, not standing out is the same as being invisible." ~ Seth Godin, The Purple Cow

NOW YOU'RE WELL-SCHOOLED IN THE GOOD, bad and the ugly aspects of this new world. Congrats for getting this far—you are one of the committed ones and this will serve you well.

Everyone who is connected to the industry—and the modern world—understands that our methods of communication and connection are changing significantly. Not everyone uses Twitter or Facebook, but surely everyone knows that they *exist*.

So why has our industry been so slow to adapt to this new era of social connection and selling? It seems only natural that companies whose specialty is person-to-person relationships would have jumped on this movement early on and embraced it.

Hesitation = Deprivation

One reason the industry may have hesitated is that no one thought it was "real." After all, we had seen it all before. Fads come and fads go. It's hard to count on something if you don't know how permanent it's going to be.

We see a lot of fads in our industry, so we might be forgiven if we assumed that social media was going to be more of the same. Companies that stuck to the tried-and-true have in the past succeeded more often than those who chased the shiny new thing.

Take the ecommerce craze in the late 90s as an example. A few direct sellers jumped right in. They built these huge computer systems, threw their catalogs online, and tried to recruit that way.

A few FTC actions later, the companies who had tried it were failing, and most of the industry was realizing that online marketing was neither an opportunity nor a threat to the way we do business. It was just a fad, and it wasn't worth our time. When social media came around, our red flags went up – was this more of the same?

Another reason for hesitation may have been just plain old fear. Fear of the unknown, new, and of untested technology. As we've seen, the Internet can be wild and uncontainable.

But you're not reading this book to find more excuses to avoid social media. You're here because you're ready to try something new. So if fear of the unknown, and fear of putting your company "out there," was holding you back, how do you get past that? How do you move forward into Social Selling?

It's Beautiful Outside

I had an interesting conversation with my six-year-old daughter recently. I found her on a beautiful Saturday, sitting and reading in her room. I peeked out the window at the glorious, sunny day, and asked her, "Honey, why don't you go and play outside?"

She looked up from her book and said, "It might rain, and I don't want to get my clothes wet."

I pointed out the window and said, "Well, honey, it's not raining now."

She looked up at me and said, "But Daddy, it *might* rain."

I pointed out the window once more and said, "But it's absolutely beautiful outside, you should take a look." It was a bright, cheerful day, and I thought that she should be outside enjoying it.

My daughter didn't even glance out the window, though. Instead, she looked at me with a very serious expression and said, "Thanks, Daddy, but I'm going to wait and see how this rain thing plays out."

Change as Opportunity

I get it. Really, I do. Some people want to wait and see how this social media thing "plays out," and that's fine. After all, it might rain! Something might go wrong!

What's worse (or better) is that this new world might change us.

Given what I've shared with you in this book, the incredible statistics, the amazing pace of technology, and the signs all around us, I think it's time to admit that social media isn't going anywhere.

Connectivity isn't just the way of the future … *it's the way of the present.* And that means that we need to get with the times and embrace it, both in our personal and professional lives.

This is *our* time.

The Real ROI Of Social Media

> "The ROI of social media is...you will still
> be in business in five years."
> Erik Qualman, Socialnomics

It's not just individuals who are resistant to change, but entire organizations – big, successful, famous, brand-name organizations who worry that changing to meet the demands of consumer technology might be too much for their organizations to deal with.

I have specific examples that I won't name here – household names in the direct selling industry, who have hundreds of thousands of distributors yet *zero* social presence, other than what their distributors and third-parties happily and perilously create on their own.

When the venerable, old-fashioned CEOs and managers of these companies eventually pass on, their companies, sadly, are likely to pass on as well. They will have done nothing to attract the next generation or keep themselves relevant and competitive in this new world.

I fear that, in the near future, several *institutions* in this industry —the companies we believed would live forever—will be gone, due to little more than willful ignorance of these new, inevitable realities.

But open-minded, ready-for-whatever professionals like you, people who seek out and read this type of book, you are actually setting the competitive stage.

You're the ones who will take your companies into the new age.

You'll grow and change and adapt and ride the Social Selling wave into the new world.

And not just survive, but truly thrive.

About the Author

Jonathan Gilliam is president and founder of Momentum Factor, a marketing and social media consulting firm serving direct selling companies exclusively.

Jonathan is a leader in the areas of marketing and social media for direct sellers. A co-founder and former Chief Marketing Officer of a successful direct selling company, he was one of the first direct sellers in the industry to build a social media presence and has since helped many of the best-known names in the industry in the areas of marketing, social media and reputation management.

Before dedicating his career to Direct Selling, Jonathan served as a senior national marketing manager for the global corporate consulting firm Deloitte, was an account director of a Top 50 Interactive marketing firm, and was the founder and CEO of HushMail, an Internet security company based in Dublin, Ireland.

On a personal note, Jonathan lives in Austin, Texas where he and his wife are raising three little girls. He says he is "totally outnumbered" — even the pet fish in his house are female.

Join Us at:

www.MomoFactor.com

www.facebook.com/momentumfactor

www.twitter.com/momofactor

www.linkedin.com/in/jonathangilliam

www.youtube.com/momofactor

Subscribe to the *MomoNews* newsletter for industry executives at our website!

Hire Jonathan to speak at your next event.

Jonathan's captivating presentation will inspire your field in the areas of Social Selling and train them how to do it right so everyone wins. His speaking style is fun, humor laden, energetic, and personal. For speaking references send him a quick email at Jonathan@MomoFactor.com about speaking at your next convention.

About Momentum Factor

"In my opinion, values are more than simple statements like 'we have integrity' or 'we put our client first.' Our values represent powerful ideas about who we are as a firm and how we make decisions under uncertainty or duress, and importantly, what we would give up if we had to make a choice." ~ Jonathan Gilliam

Our mission is to provide best-in-class marketing & management services to the world's finest direct selling companies and field leaders. Our firm works to maximize performance for clients by increasing revenue, protecting brands, engaging field & customers, and multiplying Momentum. Most of all, our aim is to become high-value, indispensible partners with our clients for the long term.

Marketing Leadership for Direct Sellers

- Complete Social Media Management
- Online Marketing and Lead Generation
- Website Design & Development
- Social Media Training for the Field
- Speakers Bureau on Topics Of Social Media and

Mobility
- Strategic Marketing
- Startup, Launch and Growth Consulting
- Automated Compliance Monitoring
- Online Reputation Repair & Protection
- World-class Marketing Strategies
- Direct Selling Video and Multimedia
- Email Marketing Campaigns

> **"**We develop 'best-in-class' programs for our clients and manage them on an ongoing basis. Rather then drop off a report, or a training session, or 'strategy,' we work with our clients to build their platforms, and their culture, to respect and leverage the power of Social Selling to not only build their following but bring a return on their investment.**"**

CORE VALUES

1. We believe that we're here to make a difference by helping the companies who help people.
2. We choose to work with clients where we can make a significant contribution.
3. We believe in simplicity versus complexity, clarity over obtuseness.
4. We covet only projects that are truly important and meaningful to our clients and us.
5. We believe in collaboration with our clients and partners, driving quality and innovation.
6. We don't settle for anything less than honesty, integrity and excellence.
7. We value family, friendship, community and spirit.

Please contact me if I can be of service!

Jonathan Gilliam
9600 Great Hills Trail Suite 150 West
Austin, Texas 78759
+1 512.994.4646
jonathan@momofactor.com
www.MomoFactor.com

MomentumFactor
The Success Multiplier for Direct Sellers

CPSIA information can be obtained at www.ICGtesting.com
Printed in the USA
BVOW081257071212

307590BV00009B/94/P